Modern 12 Step Recovery

Modern 12 Step Recovery

Glenn Rader

Maze Publishing

Copyright and Disclaimer

© 2021 by Maze Publishing

All rights reserved. No part of this book may be reproduced or transmitted in any form or by any means, graphic, electronic, or mechanical, including photocopying, recording, or by any information storage retrieval process, without the written permission of the author.

The information in this book is not intended or implied to be a substitute for advice from professionals with academic credentials and experience in the fields of addiction diagnosis and treatment or psychology. The contents of this book represent the author's opinions based on his experience as a successful recovering addict in Alcoholics Anonymous and research on the subject.

This book is not an official publication of Alcoholics Anonymous (AA). AA materials and references used in the preparation of this book are in the public domain.

ISBN: 979 - 8574281987

Hard copy and E-book versions are available at:

www.amazon.com

For general information and questions,
please send an email to:

info@mazepublishing.com

> It is a simple program
> for complicated people!
>
> Anonymous

This book is dedicated to the wonderful people who share their experience, strength, and hope to help others find a path out of addiction. Special thanks to Karen Bartos for her inspiration and support.

Table of Contents

Section	Page
- Introduction	1
- Perspective on Addiction	5
- Fundamentals of Recovery	14
- Alcoholics Anonymous (AA)	22
- The 12 Steps	31
- Psychology of the 12 Steps	41
- Recommended Action Plan	60
- Working Guide for the 12 Steps	73
- Appendix	93
- Bibliography	124
- About the Author	128

Introduction

The 12 Step program of Alcoholics Anonymous (AA) has provided millions of people an opportunity for an improved lifestyle, free from the burden of their addiction. The 12 Step program provides a new set of skills and a change in your thinking and actions that make the coping mechanism provided by alcohol and drugs unnecessary. These new skills are acquired through learning and practicing the 12 Steps as a participant in AA's unmatched international mutual support network.

The 12 Step program is an outstanding addiction recovery option for people seeking help in the fast-paced, demanding social and work environment of today. It is highly flexible because of the availability of meetings and the number of people willing to mentor and assist you. It is also a straightforward program, relying principally on a one-page list of 12 Steps and a set of reasonable expectations on the part of each participant.

Being flexible and straightforward does not mean that the 12 Step program is a "quick fix" for addiction. The program requires dedication and a commitment to learning and using the 12 Step principles. The reward for this work is long-term recovery from addiction, improved relationships, and an enhanced lifestyle. As they say in the AA recovery community: "It works if you work it!"

Over the decades since the beginning of AA in the 1930s, the profile of people who turn to AA for recovery has changed. There is significantly more diversity in the modern audience from a cultural, ethnic, and religious perspective. There have also been major advances in the understanding of the science and psychology of addiction and changes in spoken and written language. The combination of the demographic, scientific, and language changes has made the content of the 12 Step program difficult to embrace for some individuals in the modern audience seeking recovery from addiction.

This book, *Modern 12 Step Recovery*, was developed to change the way the AA program is presented. It is a user-friendly, secular packaging of AA that makes the program welcoming to individuals from all demographics, cultures, and beliefs. This "modernization" is achieved without making any fundamental changes to the underlying AA program. *Modern 12 Step Recovery* is 100% compatible with pursuing a program of recovery within the traditional AA mutual support network. This includes AA meetings, sponsor relationships, and other activities.

Modern 12 Step Recovery includes the following program enhancements:

- **Modern Framework** – The AA program is presented in a modern frame of reference with information from science and psychology.

- **Contemporary Language** – The 12 Steps and selected AA materials are presented with up-to-date wording and with added clarity.

- **Belief System Neutral** – The religious-sounding content of the 12 Steps has been removed to make the program more welcoming to people of all beliefs.

- **Enriched Program Activities** – A working guide for the 12 Steps, including a modern, straightforward Step 4 process, is provided to enrich the recovery experience.

- **Convenient Reference** – In a single, easy-to-read book you are provided background on AA, how the program works, details on the 12 Steps, and other supporting information.

Each section of this book should be read in the order that it is presented because the early sections provide information that supports subsequent topics.

The first two sections of *Modern 12 Step Recovery* provide a practical perspective on addiction and the fundamentals of successful recovery. These subjects are a foundation for understanding what the 12 Step program of AA accomplishes for you.

Perspective on Addiction

People who suffer from alcohol or drug addiction are normally faced with two common emotional challenges. First, they feel shame and personal failure regarding their situation because they continue using drugs or alcohol despite financial, legal, relationship, or health-related consequences. Second, they have to take on the emotional burden of people giving them advice like: "Get your act together," "Exercise some self-restraint," and "Drink more responsibly!" The feeling of personal shame and failure, combined with the unwelcomed advice from others, leaves the person with the belief that they are a weak-willed individual who lacks the character to control their impulse to use alcohol or drugs. They believe that it is a moral failing on their part.

The perception by the person suffering from the addiction, and everyone around them, that the primary issue is a lack of willpower is a seriously flawed view regarding addiction. This, and other misdirected assumptions about addiction, will cause individuals to spend years attempting to control their substance abuse by "trying harder" and "being more responsible." These strategies are met with failure because addiction is a physical and psychological disorder that cannot be addressed through the exercise of self-restraint.

Why do people struggling with addiction continue to use the same ill-fated strategies? It is their ego, the shame of continued failure, and a desire to prove to the people around them that those people are wrong about them having a "weak character." However, first and foremost, they continue using the same misguided approaches to addressing their addiction because they are misinformed regarding what addiction represents.

Technical Definitions

The following are technical definitions of addiction; one is provided by the medical field and the other from psychology. Both definitions use the technical language of their professions.

American Society of Addiction Medicine (ASAM)

"Addiction is a primary, chronic disease of brain reward, motivation, memory, and related circuitry. Dysfunction in these circuits leads to characteristic biological, psychological, social, and spiritual manifestations. This is reflected in an individual pathologically pursuing reward and/or relief by substance use and other behaviors.

"Addiction is characterized by the inability to consistently abstain, impairment in behavioral control, craving, diminished recognition of significant problems with one's behaviors and interpersonal relationships, and a dysfunctional emotional response. Like other chronic diseases, addiction could involve cycles of relapse and remission. Without treatment or engagement in recovery activities, addiction is progressive and can result in disability or premature death."

American Psychological Association (APA)

"Addiction is a chronic disorder with social, biological, psychological, and environmental factors influencing its development and maintenance. About half the risk for addiction is genetic. Genes affect the degree of reward individuals experience when initially using a substance, for example, drugs or engaging in certain behaviors like gambling. Genes also influence the way the body processes alcohol or other drugs. Heightened desire to re-experience use of the substance or behavior, potentially influenced by psychological factors (for example, stress or a history of trauma), social factors (like the use of substances by family and friends), and environmental factors (for example, the accessibility of low-cost drugs), can lead to regular use, with chronic use leading to brain changes.

"These brain changes include alterations in cortical (pre-frontal cortex) and sub-cortical (limbic system) regions involving the neuro-circuitry of reward, motivation, memory, impulse control, and judgment. This can lead to dramatic increases in cravings for a drug or activity, as well as impairments in the ability to successfully regulate this impulse, despite the knowledge and experience of many consequences related to the addictive behavior."

Looking at both the ASAM and APA definitions of addiction, it should be apparent that the medical and psychological communities consider addiction to be a serious condition. Words like *genetic*, *chronic disease*, *brain circuitry*, *and pathological* are used to describe addiction. Nowhere in these definitions is there a mention of addiction being an issue of a person lacking the willpower to "get their act together." There is nothing included in these definitions about a person being inherently bad or misbehaving or the substance abuse being a symptom of their poor character. It is a physical and psychological disorder.

The Path to Addiction

In addition to these technical views on addiction, it is beneficial to understand the sequence of events and the progression of the disease in practical terms.

The Starting Point

Before an individual is ever exposed to mind-altering substances, they can have personal characteristics that set them up to be more susceptible than others to the effects. These are the person's genetics and their emotional foundation. These were both mentioned in technical terms in the previous definitions.

- **Genetics** – There is significant research to support that an individual's brain chemistry, the physical structure of their brain, liver function, and other physical characteristics can cause them to respond to the effects of alcohol and drugs differently than others. As evidence of the genetic involvement, it is not unusual for the person to have a family history that includes addiction in other family members.

- **Emotional Foundation** – Some people are more responsive to the effects of alcohol and drugs because of their emotional needs. Looking back, many people in AA describe themselves as having self-esteem issues or "not being comfortable in their own skin." For them, the feel-good effects of mind-altering substances were easily embraced, even though many people were not aware they were using these for relief from their feelings at the time.

Initial Exposure

Most people experience their first use of mind-altering substances through recreational activities with friends, family members, or coworkers. It could be a school experience with peers, or it might occur at a family party or work function.

For some people, the occasional use of alcohol or drugs is just another part of socializing and does not result in addiction. For people with a genetic or emotional predisposition, alcohol or drugs represent something quite different: a physical and emotional coping mechanism that the person begins integrating into their day-to-day activities, often completely unaware that they are doing it.

Transitional Dependency

Following initial exposure, a person can go for years, even decades, making only gradual increases in the quantity and frequency of their use without knowing they are becoming dependent on the substance. During this period, the substance is making changes to the person's brain circuitry and function. This includes decision making and behavior surrounding their use of the substance.

To support their addiction, the individual begins associating with others like themselves and making other changes in their lives to facilitate using alcohol or drugs. Their new "friends" provide a social circle that supports their alcohol or drug use and who "care" about them, fulfilling a basic emotional need. As the addiction progresses, the person begins taking advantage of people with whom they have a close relationship (parents, siblings, and friends) for money and other support.

Delusional Thinking and Behavior

When a person reaches this stage in their addiction, the relationship with the substance becomes the most important thing in their lives. This pushes school, family, career, and other responsibilities into the background. The person will use alcohol or drugs despite the consequences and in contradiction to their most fundamental values, morals, and ethics.

To push the increasing guilt and shame relating to their alcohol and drug use aside, and at the same time justify their continued use, the individual will begin to exhibit delusional thinking and the related behavior. At this stage, it is more than making occasional excuses or trying to dance around the subject of their addiction with clever talk. At this point, the person behaves as if they mean what they are saying. This includes denying they have a problem, minimizing the seriousness of their situation, and blaming others for their circumstances. Many people in recovery from addiction will tell you they had no idea they were conducting themselves in this extreme and delusional manner. As one AA participant astutely described it, the addiction had stripped them of their "common sense."

Crossing the Line

Looking back, most people in recovery will tell you that at some point, things seemed to get dramatically worse. It was as if they had "crossed a line." On the other side of that line, the use of alcohol or drugs took on a different level of importance, the same priority as, perhaps, breathing.

Research in this area supports that through prolonged use of a substance, it is eventually reclassified by the brain as a survival action. As a survival action, it does not require pondering or assessment before doing it. In other words, the person's day-to-day functioning requires the substance, and they use it without any decision-making. The behavior and related negative results are not even considered. Telling the person to stop using is like telling them to stop breathing.

Living an Alternative Reality

After crossing the line, and with the mind-altering substances integrated into their day-to-day physical and psychological processes, the individual begins to behave as if they are oblivious to what is really going on. In an environment of increasing consequences and a deteriorating quality of life, the person continues living in the addiction—it is their new reality.

Fundamentals of Recovery

As indicated in the previous section, addiction is not simply an issue of being weak-willed and lacking the character to control the intake of alcohol or drugs. It is not something that can be addressed by simply exercising self-restraint over the quantity and frequency of use. Addiction is a primary, chronic disease of brain reward, motivation, memory, and physical issues. Recovery from addiction requires treatment of the underlying physical and psychological causes to be effective.

To experience long-term recovery success, four important dimensions of addiction must be addressed on the path to recovery. These are self-direction, abstinence, physical health maintenance, and a cognitive-behavioral transformation. A program of addiction recovery that embraces each of these dimensions has a higher probability of success. Single dimension attempts are typically plagued with relapse and are unsuccessful.

Self-Direction

The starting point for effective addiction recovery is for the individual to take personal responsibility for their own success. Being self-directed means putting the bruised ego and shame associated with the addiction behind them and acting responsibly. This does not mean doing it on their own. The process of self-direction begins with surrendering to the fact that they are incapable of addressing the addiction and that they need to access professionals and a support structure for guidance.

The need for the individual to be self-directed as a major driver of successful recovery is described in the Working Definition of Recovery published by the U.S. Substance Abuse and Mental Health Services Administration (SAMHSA). Paraphrasing from this publication:

"An important factor in the recovery process is the presence and involvement of people who believe in the person's ability to recover; who offer hope, support, and encouragement; and who also suggest strategies and resources for change. [However,] self-direction is the foundation for recovery as individuals define their own life goals and design their unique path towards those goals."

Self-direction goes beyond simply taking the initial action to seek out help or accept the help that is being offered. It means being committed to following the suggestions that are made by the recovery community and viewing the process as a long-term pursuit of personal growth and development.

Caution must be exercised because even if the person accepts that they might have a problem, the addictive thinking will direct them to ineffective solutions. The addicted brain will feed them an endless stream of bad choices like cutting back to only drinking on weekends, limiting consumption to only two beers a day, or marking their bottles so they know how much they are drinking. All of these allow the person to continue using while creating the illusion that they are taking action. These actions may even get a few people "off their back," but this is not the meaning of self-directed recovery.

Abstinence

The second prerequisite to beginning effective recovery, something that is mission-critical to the process, is to permanently abstain from using mind-altering substances of any form. This includes alcohol, marijuana, prescription opiates, cocaine, heroin, or anything with addictive properties. Abstinence helps to ensure that whatever physical changes present in the brain and other body functions can begin to heal and to mitigate further damage. Having a "clear head," free from the effects of alcohol and drugs, is also essential for learning the AA principles and realizing the benefits of the 12 Step program. Complete abstinence is advocated by science and psychology.

A logical question to pose at this point is: "How is the person supposed to abstain from using when their problem seems to be their inability to abstain from using?" The answer to this question lies directly in the addiction version of abstaining versus the recovery version.

Abstinence to the person suffering from addiction is normally viewed as a process that is done in isolation and without any support. One of the principal benefits of engaging in the AA network early in recovery is the world-class support you get for abstinence. Being active in meetings, working with a sponsor, and otherwise being engaged in productive recovery-oriented activities has proven to be an effective support mechanism for abstaining from using in the early stages of recovery. Short-term prescription medication is also available to assist in early abstinence.

Another appropriate question is: "Can a person return to being a normal, recreational user of alcohol and drugs at some point?" The response to this question from people in the AA recovery community is a resounding "NO!" Why?

Because the risk of returning to your original addicted state, and even something more advanced, is very high. It is simply not worth taking a life-threatening gamble of returning to the use of mind-altering substances. Killing yourself or others in a car accident, permanent chemical brain damage, and life-long incarceration are all potential outcomes of the decision to return to using alcohol or drugs.

A person who has been using mind-altering substances heavily should not try to abstain from using these on their own. They should get a professional assessment of their situation from an addiction treatment center or addiction therapist before attempting to quit. Self-managed withdrawal (detox) without professional medical supervision can be life-threatening.

Physical Health Maintenance

The third key area that requires attention as part of the recovery process is health maintenance. Alcohol and drug abuse have been shown to be involved in more than 200 diseases and health-related issues. Even if an individual is not showing symptoms of these, underlying changes in body chemistry and the immune system are occurring that will put the person in a compromised position eventually. Several of the major health issues caused by alcohol and drug abuse are highlighted below.

Brain Related – Disruption of communication pathways, changes in the physical structure of the brain, memory loss, deterioration of attention span, and learning disabilities.

Heart – Cardiomyopathy (heart muscle issues), irregular heartbeat, stroke, and high blood pressure.

Liver – Cirrhosis of the liver, steatosis (fatty liver), alcoholic hepatitis, and fibrosis.

Pancreas – Pancreatitis resulting from toxins produced in the pancreas.

Cancer – Throat, mouth, larynx, breast, liver, colorectal, and esophageal cancer.

Abstinence is effective in removing the major contributor to health issues from the equation. However, additional action is required to address the problems introduced by failing to eat regularly and a sedentary lifestyle. As a result, an important complement to other recovery activities is improved nutrition and physical activity. Even small changes in these areas can have a significant impact on the health maintenance dimension of recovery.

Cognitive-Behavioral Change

The fourth area, and the primary focus of the 12 Step program, is to transform the thinking (cognition) and emotions and actions (behaviors) that are behind the addiction. Without this transformation, the reason for needing the coping mechanism represented by the alcohol and drugs will remain. In the words of the recovery community, a change in your "stinking thinking" is critical because "the same person will drink again."

Attempts at addressing the addiction by simply abstaining and focusing on a few physical health improvements, without working on the cognitive-behavioral aspects of recovery, will be met with failure. Those people who just stop "cold turkey" from using alcohol and drugs, and do not address the cognitive-behavioral element, are said to have "white-knuckle" sobriety. This is a metaphor for having to clench their fists to avoid taking a drink just to make it through each day. These people use the white-knuckle approach as if they were practicing some form of "advanced willpower" to stop their use of drugs and alcohol. Instead, they need to acquire new tools for coping that are provided through a cognitive-behavioral transformation. Without this change in thinking and behavior, the lifestyle of a white-knuckle recovering person will be miserable and lacking any real quality of life.

In the end, the propensity to relapse is very high for those who take the white-knuckle approach. This relapse might occur using an alternative to alcohol and drugs that represents a new coping mechanism. Included in these alternatives could be over-eating, gambling, shopping, sex, or co-dependency, each of these being used to push personal problems and obligations into the background. All of these alternative addictions come with unwelcome consequences. What they also have in common is that the path out of each is the same: a change in the person's thinking and behavior.

Alcoholics Anonymous (AA)

What is AA?

AA is an international support network of people engaged in helping each other to recover from alcohol and drug addiction, maintain sobriety, and enjoy an improved quality of life. AA accomplishes this using a unique organization, mutual support structure, and the 12 Steps to facilitate the cognitive-behavioral change in a person.

AA was founded by Bill Wilson and Dr. Bob Smith in Akron, Ohio, in 1935. Both men were hopeless alcoholics who discovered a path to sobriety that would become the foundation of AA. The innovation in addiction recovery that Wilson and Smith crafted was based on their experiences with a spiritual self-help group called the Oxford Group, personal insight gained through their own recovery from alcoholism, and working with other alcoholics. The 12 Steps of AA, the unique AA mutual support structure, and a sustainable, self-funded organization were all part of this innovation. Today, AA has a global presence with participation exceeding 2.1 million. The principal reference book of AA, *Alcoholics Anonymous* (the "Big Book"), has sold more than 35 million copies and is available in 71 languages. The program has also been adopted for other addictions including gambling, eating, smoking, sex, and co-dependency (Al-Anon).

Everyone is welcome to participate in AA regardless of ethnicity, culture, gender identity, and spiritual beliefs, including agnostics and atheists. There are no requirements to participate in AA except a sincere desire to address your addiction. Although originally intended to have a singleness of purpose–helping alcoholics–the participants in today's AA include people who struggle with addictions to mind-altering substances of all forms, many with cross addictions to multiple substances. AA is funded through voluntary contributions by participants; there are no dues or fees.

The AA program operates based on personal anonymity (privacy) of all those involved. Sharing at the AA meetings and in other activities is done on a first-name basis only. Revealing any additional details of your identity, work, outside interests, and other facts about you is completely at your discretion. In support of this anonymity, no information is provided to the press, television, radio, films, or social media regarding AA or any of its participants.

AA does not have any involvement with businesses, political organizations, religious groups, or other entities. It provides no endorsements or funding and expresses no opinions regarding the activities of outside organizations. There is no advertising, as the program operates based on the success of its participants. Maintaining anonymity, independence from the influence of outside organizations, and an attraction-not-promotion philosophy helps to ensure that AA will not be diverted from its primary purpose: helping each other to achieve and maintain sobriety.

Each group in AA is completely autonomous with respect to how it conducts its affairs and the composition of activities they undertake. The only requirements are that their activities are 12 Step-based and that they do not impact the functioning of another AA group. This autonomy and flexibility are important because this permits each AA group to have a character and makeup that serves the needs of the people in their local communities. Some more populated areas will have specialized AA groups for young people, the LGBTQ community, groups focused on reading the AA literature, meditation-oriented meetings, and other special interests. The requirement that all activities be 12 Step-based helps maintain a common thread and a central focus to recovery efforts worldwide.

AA has a central professional team called AA World Services. They are an organization that supports the global AA community. In this support capacity, they work to maintain the common mission of AA and to manage certain administrative functions, for example, the publication and distribution of AA literature. AA World Services is not involved, in any way, in directing the activities of the local AA groups. World Services obtains input from the local groups through the district and area representatives from those groups.

The Mutual Support Network

The AA mutual support network consists of meetings and other activities that are coordinated by volunteers who are also in recovery from addiction. It is this mutual support structure that has withstood the test of time for more than eighty years and is one of the most successful self-help groups in history. Mutual support was not a new concept at the time that AA was founded in the 1930s. The founding members of AA adopted this form of support for addiction recovery because it was particularly effective based on their hands-on success with it as a recovery support model.

Several mutual support activities have become common practice in AA. There will be some variations on these depending on the geographic location and local customs of the AA groups.

Mutual Support Activities

AA Meetings – These are regularly scheduled meetings for people in AA 12 Step recovery. A meeting designated as a "Closed" meeting is only open to AA participants. An "Open" meeting can be attended by anyone including family and friends. Meetings are generally held in rooms that are rented at facilities or online through video conferencing. The meetings often include the following activities:

- Meeting Administration – Selected readings, the celebration of sobriety anniversaries, local AA announcements, and other activities facilitated by a volunteer who coordinates the meeting.

- Sharing – Meeting participants share their perspectives on the 12 Steps of AA, what has been successful for them in their recovery journey, and related topics.

- Open Talks – These are presentations by people experiencing successful recovery. They share their stories regarding how they came about their addiction, what it was like living with addiction, and their path to a better lifestyle. As the name implies, these talks are normally open to everyone including AA participants, family members, and the public.

- Meeting Support – Literature libraries, coffee and snacks, and the collection of donations (usually $1 or $2 per meeting in 2021) are other parts of an AA meeting that you might observe.

To identify in-person or online AA meetings in your area, or online meetings internationally, contact a local AA office, an addiction treatment center, or search the internet.

Sponsorship – Another important function of the mutual support network is the process where someone with experience in AA works with a newcomer on a one-on-one basis as an advisor and mentor. In addition to providing general support to the newcomer, the most important role of the sponsor is to help the person work through the 12 Steps.

Service Work – As an AA participant in the mutual support process, you are encouraged to be active in the group by helping to support the group's success. Examples of these optional activities include leading a meeting, giving an open talk, making coffee, and sponsoring another person.

Conventions – There are local, state, regional, and national conventions that are open to everyone. These conventions include panel discussions, speakers, table displays, and other activities.

Special Events – There are "clean" holiday parties, excursions to local attractions, dinners, and a variety of other activities that are part of the mutual support process.

Mutual Support Benefits

By participating in the mutual support network, you are rewarded with significant benefits. It is an environment that facilitates learning the 12 Steps and promotes your personal growth and development.

- Early Recovery Support – The meetings and other activities are welcoming, provide a safe place to go, and reduce the loneliness often accompanying addiction.

- An Atmosphere of Change – Participating in a non-judgmental, friendly environment, where you can talk openly, helps to reduce stress and builds a sense of empowerment.

- A Vision of Hope – Being around people who are experiencing successful recovery and enjoying a new quality of life is motivational and provides a vision for your recovery.

- Connections – The willingness of people to give you their contact information provides an outstanding, responsive system of support outside of the meetings.

- Improved Social Life – Many people make friends with other AA participants and engage in social activities together.

- Source of Recovery Resources – AA participants are excellent sources for literature, activities, supporting therapies, and other resources to use in your recovery.

- Cost-Effectiveness – The mutual support structure, facilitated by knowledgeable non-professionals, is very cost-effective.

In 2019, it was estimated by AA World Services that there were over 125,000 AA groups in the support network internationally.

Outside the Scope of AA

There may be assistance and services that you will require as part of your program of recovery that are not provided by AA. Many people in AA recovery use one or more of these successfully to augment and complement their AA program.

AA does not provide the following services:

- Assessment – Medical or psychological evaluation and determination of the appropriate treatment.

- Detox — Medically supervised withdrawal from a substance (called detoxification or detox).

- In-Patient Treatment — Many of the treatment centers use 12 Step recovery as a part of their program. However, there are no treatment centers owned and operated by AA.

- Psychological Therapy — Professional one-on-one or group therapy administered by a licensed professional.

- Nutrition Counseling — Guidance on improved eating habits and associated changes in a person's diet.

- Financial Support — Financial assistance, advice, or services including housing, clothing, money, and transportation.

- Job Assistance — Identification of job opportunities or related placement services.

- Interfaces with Outside Parties — Involvement with employers, agencies, or any aspect of the legal system including lawyers, parole boards, and the courts.

If a service is not listed under the mutual support activities previously described, it is likely outside of the scope of AA. Your sponsor, or another AA participant with several years of successful recovery, should be able to address questions in this area as well.

The 12 Steps

The 12 Steps of AA are the focal point of the AA program and all of the activities of the mutual support network. The Steps represent a sequence of information, learning, and actions to affect a transformation in your thinking and behavior.

Historical Perspective

The development of the 12 Steps and mutual support network was preceded by other social movements and scientific efforts in the United States that were targeted at addressing alcoholism. A historical perspective on these other treatment efforts is interesting and provides a broader context for understanding the 12 Steps. Here are several examples from the period 1784-1930.

- Benjamin Rush, M.D. – He popularized the concept that

alcoholism was a disease and treated it by inducing vomiting, frightening the patient, drawing large amounts of blood, and other methods (ca. 1784).

- Temperance Movement – This group focused on activities designed to raise public awareness about the benefits of drinking in moderation. Eventually, they altered their approach to advocate total abstinence, rather than just moderation, as the only viable path to recovery (ca. 1800).

- Washingtonian Movement – This group added the concept of having the alcoholic share their experiences publicly as an important part of the path to personal freedom and to promote public awareness (ca. 1840).

- Fraternal Temperance Societies / Reform Clubs – These were mutual support groups established to help each other in private. These groups brought the concept of anonymity to the scene of addiction treatment. Some groups even had secret passwords and handshakes (ca. 1840).

- Inebriate Facilities – These were large, medically run facilities that were operated by alcoholism specialists. They offered detox, residential services, day treatment, and outpatient care services, versions of which are widely used today (ca. 1870).

- Miracle Cures – These were potions and elixirs to cure alcoholism. Many contained a high percentage of alcohol (ca. 1880).

- Religious Conversion – These were missions and other organizations that helped alcoholics to improve their lifestyle through religious affiliation.

- Physical Treatment – This included electroshock therapy, surgical lobotomies, sterilization, drugs, diets, exercise, work, and many other approaches.

- Psychological Care – These physicians and therapists approached alcoholism from the standpoint that a personal psychosis or disordered personality was the cause, and that unmanageable alcohol consumption was a symptom of the illness.

- Prohibition – A national law that was passed to make the production and sale of alcohol illegal in the United States (1920-1933).

Where many of these approaches had successful elements, they were not effective in providing a foundation for long-term recovery. The AA program was an advancement in addiction treatment because it introduced a combination of abstinence, personal transformation, and maintenance that promoted sustained recovery. The 12 Steps are an integral part of that process.

Development of the 12 Steps

With many great discoveries, there is usually someone with the insight, intuition, intellectual capacity, and correct timing to put all the pieces of the puzzle together into a working model. As it relates to recovery from alcohol addiction in the 1930s, that person was Bill Wilson.

Wilson was known to be highly intelligent, with an eclectic, unique approach to problem-solving. He was an original thinker with a "big picture" perspective. In his youth, Wilson was president of his senior class, an accomplished athlete, and team captain, and he taught himself to play the violin while in high school. Following high school, his mother, a doctor, worked to help him get into the Massachusetts Institute of Technology (MIT). He failed the entrance exam. He was offered a position with Thomas Edison at Menlo Park based on exceptional test scores, but he did not accept. Wilson also completed a law school education but never practiced law. He found some success as an investment advisor, but this, and the other opportunities mentioned above, were believed to have been compromised by his alcoholism.

When Wilson emerged from his addiction, he turned his intellectual capacity and vision toward developing a path to recovery for alcoholics. In the early stages of AA, Wilson and other alcoholics participated in a group called the Oxford Group. He was directed to the Oxford Group by a friend who had experienced recovery by practicing the group's core principles. These principles were designed to help its participants, which included alcoholics, to improve their quality of life. Several of the Oxford principles became important elements of the AA program including developing an understanding of your personal "defects," sharing these with another person, making restitution to those who you had impacted with your behavior, and seeking guidance through meditation, reflection, and prayer. The AA program also adopted several of the Oxford Group's organization principles that were designed to minimize the influence of, or obligation to, outside parties.

Bill Wilson and several others broke away from the Oxford Group over certain Oxford practices. These included the Oxford Group being too aggressive and coercive for the suffering alcoholic, public "witnessing" that did not fit the alcoholic's shy nature, and issues regarding who could participate in the group. Following this departure, Wilson and the others started their own mutual support group, which would eventually become AA, and began using an informal, word-of-mouth 6 Step program in their one-on-one and group sessions with alcoholics. Although there were variations on the informal Steps, Bill Wilson would later recall them as being approximately the following:

1. We admitted that we were licked, that we were powerless over alcohol.
2. We made a moral inventory of our defects.
3. We confessed or shared our shortcomings with another person in confidence.
4. We made restitution to all those we had harmed by our drinking.
5. We tried to help other alcoholics, with no thought of reward in money or prestige.
6. We prayed to whatever God we thought there was for power to practice these precepts.

The final 12 Steps of AA, penned by Bill Wilson and reviewed by his "team," were published in 1939. The 12 Steps represent an expansion and refinement of the 6 Step informal program. The original 12 Steps, referred to as the Traditional 12 Steps going forward, are provided in the Appendix as a reference.

The Modern 12 Steps

The Modern 12 Steps, developed for this book, represent an evolution of the Traditional 12 Steps for the modern audience. This evolution includes updating the Traditional Steps to reflect more contemporary wording and adding clarity to their descriptions. In addition, any spiritual or religious content in the Steps has been removed. All of these enhancements were accomplished while maintaining the original intent of the Traditional Steps.

The Traditional Steps have not been updated since they were published in the 1930s. Many people in today's AA are working with their own informal translations and interpretations of the Traditional Steps to make the Steps work for them. With the assistance of other AA participants, individuals are capable of developing a perspective on the Traditional Steps that allows them to look past the dated terminology and Christian emphasis. If you ask anyone in AA today to describe what a particular Step means to them, you will get a wide variety of responses. Most of the variation will be due to their interpretations of the wording or adjustments they made for their spiritual or religious preferences.

The Modern 12 Steps were developed to make available a standardized, updated set of Steps that could be easily embraced by all newcomers and used in traditional AA meetings and other activities. As you read through the Steps on the following page, study each one closely. Ask yourself what the Step is suggesting to you as a course of action. Details on each Step are provided later in the book.

Modern 12 Steps

1. We admitted we were powerless over our addiction—that our lives had become unmanageable.

2. Came to trust that resources outside of ourselves could restore us to rational thinking and behavior.

3. Made a decision to turn our direction and actions over to the guidance of those resources.

4. Made an honest and thorough list of the issues in our lives.

5. Admitted to ourselves and another person our specific role in those issues.

6. Became entirely ready to make changes in our character.

7. Began making changes in our thinking and behavior with humility and honesty.

8. Made a list of all persons we had harmed and became willing to make amends to them all.

9. Made direct amends to those people wherever possible, except when to do so would injure them or others.

10. Continued to be aware of our thoughts and actions and when we were wrong promptly admitted it.

11. Pursued a program of ongoing self-improvement and empowerment through meditation, reflection, and study.

12. Having experienced a personal transformation as a result of these steps, we tried to carry this program to other addicts and to practice these principles in all aspects of our lives.

Modern 12 Steps
Single-Word Descriptions

Historically, single-word identifiers have been used by AA participants to describe the Steps. The following updated, single-word descriptions are used as part of *Modern 12 Step Recovery*.

Step	Description
1	Acceptance
2	Trust
3	Commitment
4	Introspection
5	Affirmation
6	Determination
7	Transformation
8	Compassion
9	Reparation
10	Diligence
11	Evolution
12	Integration

It is very effective to view each Step combined with its single-word description. This brings another level of clarity to each Step regarding what it is doing in your personal transformation.

Modern 12 Steps with Single-Word Descriptions

1. **Acceptance** – We admitted we were powerless over our addiction–that our lives had become unmanageable.

2. **Trust** – Came to trust that resources outside of ourselves could restore us to rational thinking and behavior.

3. **Commitment** – Made a decision to turn our direction and actions over to the guidance of those resources.

4. **Introspection** – Made an honest and thorough list of the issues in our lives.

5. **Affirmation** – Admitted to ourselves and another person our specific role in those issues.

6. **Determination** – Became entirely ready to make changes in our character.

7. **Transformation** – Began making changes in our thinking and behavior with humility and honesty.

8. **Compassion** – Made a list of all persons we had harmed and became willing to make amends to them all.

9. **Reparation** – Made direct amends to those people wherever possible, except when to do so would injure them or others.

10. **Diligence** – Continued to be aware of our thoughts and actions and when we were wrong promptly admitted it.

11. **Evolution** – Pursued a program of ongoing self-improvement and empowerment through meditation, reflection, and study.

12. **Integration** – Having experienced a personal transformation as a result of these steps, we tried to carry this program to other addicts and to practice these principles in all aspects of our lives.

Psychology of the 12 Steps

Bill Wilson and his collaborators developed a process that was effective in rehabilitating alcoholics through hands-on, trial-and-error work with themselves and others. In addition to the influence of the Oxford Group previously described, the AA program had casual influences from medicine and other professional fields that helped shape the 12 Steps and mutual support structure. However, the developments in AA were principally a layman's undertaking by smart, motivated, recovering alcoholics who were trying to help others with the same serious illness.

Although it was not conceived directly as a product of a professional or academic endeavor, the 12 Step program, including the sequence of the Steps and the recommendations made in each, are very contemporary from the standpoint of modern psychology. When looking at the 12 Step program through the eyes of Cognitive-

Behavioral Therapy (CBT), it is rich in the principles and techniques of CBT that are used to address misguided thinking of many forms including depression, anxiety, addiction, and other disorders. The 12 Step program's success and longevity are evidence of its fundamental soundness from a CBT standpoint.

The purpose of this section of *Modern 12 Step Recovery* is to provide the perspective of modern psychology to improve your understanding of what the AA program does for you. The additional perspective from psychology is also intellectually engaging to learn about and provides a basis for seeking additional information on personal development that will complement your 12 Step work.

The AA Innovation

In the Big Book of AA, and with great insight, AA identifies that the underlying cause of addiction is the person's selfish, self-centered personality, a defensive personality motivated by low self-esteem. Quoting from the Big Book of AA:

"Selfishness-self-centeredness! That, we think, is the root of our troubles. Driven by a hundred forms of fear, self-delusion, self-seeking, and self-pity, we step on the toes of our fellows and they retaliate."

Interpreting this statement by AA, the central issue of the

alcoholic is problematic thinking that is grounded in fear, self-delusion, self-seeking, and self-pity. To defend against these insecurities, the person develops a selfish, self-centered way of addressing relationships with the people, places, and things around them. In today's recovery community, and with some irony, the person just described is referred to as an "ego-maniac with a self-esteem complex."

The response by the world to the self-centered person is negative—certainly not one filled with the support, praise, and accolades sought by the person to bolster their confidence. The disapproving response by people further fuels the underlying self-esteem issues. The "quick fix" to the situation is alcohol and drugs, or other avoidance-based coping mechanisms, to escape the situation. It is difficult to see yourself as the self-centered person just described when you first enter recovery. Why? Because it is difficult to see yourself as being self-centered when you are self-centered!

To address what AA considered to be the root of the addiction issue, "selfishness-self-centeredness," it was believed that some form of "psychic change" would be required. However, before the advent of AA, how to go about affecting that "psychic change" was elusive to both the fields of medicine and psychology. The innovation that AA brought to addiction recovery was a process for facilitating that change.

In the early 1930s, and after breaking away from the Oxford Group, the founding members of AA began using the Step-based process for addiction recovery with alcoholics. Based on observing the success of this firsthand, Dr. Silkworth, who was the chief of medicine at a leading addiction treatment hospital, declared the new program to be a significant breakthrough in the field of addiction treatment, a process for affecting the required "psychic change." Silkworth became an outspoken advocate of the program, even staking his professional reputation on this new approach to addiction recovery. When you have completed reading this chapter, The Doctor's Opinion, taken directly from the Big Book of AA, is provided in the Appendix. It is a historically significant statement by Dr. Silkworth regarding the AA innovation.

How the 12 Step program helps you to achieve the personal transformation, the "psychic change," is described in general terms in the AA literature. However, these are layman's descriptions of the change process, not insights directly grounded in psychological theory or practice. Today, we have the benefit of more than eighty years of research into the psychology of thinking and behavior to draw from to get a better understanding of why the 12 Step program has been effective for people.

The ABCs of Change

The contemporary fields of psychology called Rational Emotive Behavioral Therapy (REBT) and Cognitive-Behavioral Therapy (CBT) provide a wealth of insight into what the 12 Step program is doing for you toward a personal transformation. Dr. Albert Ellis, the founder of REBT, and Dr. Aaron T. Beck, the developer of CBT, ushered in these new forms of psychotherapy beginning in the 1950s. Both therapies, referred to collectively as CBT going forward, are targeted at cultivating open-minded, flexible thinking and actions in an individual. This new cognitive flexibility replaces the dysfunctional thinking that is at the center of addiction and other disorders. CBT has been widely researched and empirically tested for validity.

The ABC model of CBT is used to describe the thinking, emotional, and behavioral problems of individuals who suffer from addiction, depression, and other disorders. It is a very effective model for illustrating what the 12 Step program is accomplishing for you from the perspective of modern psychology.

> **A = Activating Event:** An external or internal event that initiates the thought process. An example of an external event would be a co-worker telling you that you are not a nice person. An example of an internal event is reminding yourself that you need to take your car in for

repair.

B = Beliefs: Deeply held beliefs, assumptions, expectations, and automatic thoughts that you use to interpret external and internal events. An example of this would be an unconscious, deeply held belief by you that people's opinions of you are critical to your well-being.

C = Consequences: These are emotions and behaviors that result from your interpretation of events using your beliefs. Example: (A) Your co-worker tells you that you are not a nice person. (B) You believe that approval by others is an important determining factor in your self-worth. (C) You react as if what they are saying is a fact. You feel dejected, sad, and do your best to avoid them in the future.

Individuals who have an inflexible, negative perspective about the world, themselves, and others will have unhealthy emotional and behavioral outcomes when they interpret events in their lives. Low self-esteem and a self-centered, defensive, and impulsive manner of living, as described by the AA founders, is predictable with this "stinking thinking." The alternative, healthy version of the "You are not a nice person" ABC scenario will be illustrated later in this section. It is important to reinforce that if you are struggling with addiction, you should not be too quick to conclude that the person with the unhealthy thinking process described in the ABC scenario above is not you. These thinking issues present themselves in many different forms in people. To repeat an earlier observation: "It is difficult to see yourself as self-centered when you are self-centered."

Cognitive Distortions

Based on research by Dr. Beck and popularized by Dr. David D. Burns, there are ten "thinking errors," called cognitive distortions, that are commonly used by people to interpret events. These distortions are present in people suffering from addiction, depression, and other thinking-based disorders. The results of this distorted thinking are unhealthy emotions and responses to events. Consider each of the cognitive distortions in the list below carefully. These can become routine in a person suffering from addiction.

Cognitive Distortions

1. **All-Or-Nothing Thinking** – Thinking in extremes; no room for grey areas.

2. **Overgeneralization** – Based on a single occurrence, you conclude that it will continue to repeat.

3. **Mental Filtering** – Focusing only on the negative aspects of things and ignoring the positive.

4. **Disqualifying the Positive** – Discounting positive experiences. They do not count for one reason or

another.

5. **Mind Reading / Fortune Telling** – Jumping to the conclusion that the outcome will be negative without supporting facts.

6. **Catastrophizing (Magnification)** – Dwelling on the worst-or best-case scenario occurring because of a single event.

7. **Emotional Reasoning** – Believing that if I feel this way, it must be true.

8. **Shoulds** – Self-defeating attempts to motivate ourselves and others with unrealistic expectations, only to ultimately feel a sense of failure when these expectations are not met.

9. **Labeling** – Extreme generalization. I am a loser versus I made a mistake.

10. **Personalization and Blame** – Blaming yourself or others for situations that you do not have control over.

Avoidance-Based Solutions

Unaware that you are operating with an inflexible, unhealthy set of beliefs and distortions, you develop various strategies and actions for avoiding unpleasant situations, thoughts, and emotions rather than addressing these in a fact-based, objective manner. These solutions might include dodging uncomfortable situations with people, places, and things, procrastinating, and engaging in other activities that will keep you from having to face your day-to-day issues. The avoidance-based actions might also include gambling, sex, shopping, eating, and, central to this book, the use of alcohol and drugs. All of these provide a distraction and obsession to help you cope by avoiding reality.

Avoidance-based solutions represent short-term, "quick fix" actions that make the overall situation worse, often impacting other areas of your life and the people around you. The additional issues caused by using an avoidance approach feed the "stinking thinking" and make the situation worse.

The "Psychic Change"

Looking through the eyes of modern psychology, the 12 Step program helps to facilitate a change in the way you approach your ABC thinking and actions. The 12 Step program transforms you from being a person working with rigid, inflexible beliefs, cognitive distortions, and avoidance-based coping strategies to a new way of living grounded in awareness, flexible thinking, and healthy emotions and behaviors.

To illustrate this shift in thinking and behavior, it is effective to use the earlier "You are not a nice person" ABC scenario with an alternative, healthy outcome. Example: (A) Your co-worker tells you that you are not a nice person. (B) You consider the specific facts and the context of their remark and the possible alternative explanations for their comment. (C) Based on this objective assessment, you determine that, in this instance, you were being inappropriately aggressive and demanding and that an apology to the person is appropriate. You make the amend with them, then you let it go!

The example above is very different than the original scenario where your interpretation of the person's comment was based on a deeply held belief about the importance of people's opinions. Then, through a distorted "generalization" of their comment, you concluded that you are not a nice person overall, let it impact you all day, and allowed it to influence your relationship with the person going forward.

To achieve this change in your thinking and behavior, the 12 Step program provides a new set of tools for navigating life. Here is a description of what working through the 12 Steps and participating in the mutual support network provides, expressed using the perspective of CBT.

The CBT of AA

1. Personal Empowerment
2. Integrity
3. Cognitive Flexibility
4. Mindfulness
5. Collaboration
6. Self-Discovery
7. Action Emphasis
8. Purposeful Repetition

Personal Empowerment

The 12 Step program causes a paradigm shift, a fundamental change, in the way you conduct yourself and interact with the people, places, and things around you. Referred to as personal empowerment, a core principle in CBT, this begins with you taking responsibility for your life, having a realistic view of your circumstances, and making informed decisions. An important dimension to personal empowerment is taking ownership of the problems that you create and holding yourself accountable, not blaming others.

Personal empowerment does not mean simply motivating yourself to get things done. It means being proactive, taking charge of your life, and working with the best people and information you have available to better yourself and others. Personal empowerment is also not the same as willpower, which is simply exerting control to do something or to restrain impulses. For example, you could try using willpower to achieve "white-knuckle" sobriety as an approach to recovery. Being empowered relative to your addiction means admitting and accepting that you do not have control over your addiction and then taking the responsible step of getting outside of yourself and accessing resources to address the issue.

Integrity

The 12 Step program helps you to improve your overall level of integrity. Integrity includes the personal traits of being honest, open, and having strong moral and ethical convictions. Conducting life with integrity has a major impact on your interactions with others and the decision making that takes place in your ABC process. Improved integrity drives your interpretation of events, emotions, and behaviors in a productive and positive direction.

Addiction presents a challenge to all dimensions of a person's integrity. Maintaining an addictive lifestyle places demands on a person to be dishonest and secretive and to compromise their moral and ethical qualities. Even if your integrity was at a world-class level before developing an addiction, the acts of hiding your use of mind-altering substances, making excuses for alcohol- or drug-induced behavior, and other aspects of your addiction can leave you "bankrupt" in integrity.

In the 12 Step program, work on both personal empowerment and integrity begins with Step 1 and continues throughout the entire 12 Step program.

Cognitive Flexibility

One of the significant contributions of the 12 Step program is to facilitate cognitive flexibility in a person. Cognitive flexibility is the human capacity to consider alternatives and determine a course of action based on the facts of the situation at hand. Expressed in the context of the ABC model, cognitive flexibility influences how you perceive events and interpret those events, and the emotional and behavioral responses that result. People who have solid cognitive flexibility exhibit several important traits. These include the ability to suspend judgment, weigh evidence, consider options, have preferences (not absolutes), to be skeptical about first thoughts, and to resist reacting impulsively.

As previously described, the environment of addiction is grounded in inflexible thinking using rigid, fixed beliefs, assumptions, and negative automatic thoughts about the world, yourself, and others. The abuse of alcohol and drugs impacts the brain's executive function, which includes working memory, processing capacity, and self-control. The executive function manages your skills relating to processing diverse concepts, considering alternatives, and making informed choices. Inflexible thinking results from the loss of executive function.

Regaining cognitive flexibility starts with complete abstinence from mind-altering substances as a part of Step 1. Then, with Steps 2 and 3, you begin to improve your cognitive flexibility by turning your attention to external resources for alternatives and guidance regarding your addiction. Improvements in your cognitive flexibility, combined with growth in your personal empowerment and integrity, are a powerful combination for success in recovery.

Mindfulness

Mindfulness is the self-management of being fully present and engaged in the moment. It means being aware of your environment, thoughts, and emotions, without judgment or distraction. It is a central tenet of modern psychology. Another way to view mindfulness is to think of yourself as being an impartial "observer" of your own thoughts, emotions, and actions. In a sense, it is viewing yourself as two people, one who is thinking and the other who is objectively viewing the thinking. The 12 Step program helps to cultivate the skill of being mindful.

Being mindful is the starting point for effective cognitive flexibility because it positions you for being present and objective about how you interpret the events in your life and the subsequent actions you take. Being mindful means not having a head cluttered with past events, ruminating about how things could have been, or having unhealthy thoughts about the future that consume you in unwarranted fear.

The 12 Step program challenges you with being mindful at various stages. This includes the work with your sponsor in Steps 4 and 5, in Step 10 as a part of the self-monitoring process, and in Step 11 as a part of continuous improvement through meditation and reflection. Mindfulness is also enhanced by your participation in the AA meetings as you listen to other people sharing their experience, strength, and hope.

Collaboration

Collaboration is the process of two or more people working toward a common goal. It is an essential attribute of the relationship between the therapist and client in the history of psychology and at the center of the success of the 12 Step program.

As a part of the mutual support process of AA, you are provided several opportunities to participate in collaborative relationships that are open, honest, and non-judgmental. This includes discussions at your AA meetings, work with your sponsor on the 12 Steps, and eventually in your role as a sponsor helping another person. These collaborative relationships help you gain personal empowerment, integrity, and cognitive flexibility.

A critical aspect of all of these collaborations is that the people in AA have firsthand experience with your issue and the willingness to help you stay objective and fact-based about what you are saying and doing. In simpler terms, these people are willing to "let you know" if what they are hearing is addictive thinking or if you are on the right track.

Self-Discovery

Self-discovery or introspection, the process of looking at yourself objectively, is a part of both CBT and the 12 Step program. Where mindfulness involves being aware and discerning, self-discovery is focused on uncovering deeply held beliefs, assumptions, and negative automatic thoughts that are influencing your misdirected emotions and behaviors.

As part of Steps 4 and 5, you are directly involved in guided self-discovery with a sponsor. The work on these Steps involves listing the issues in your life, but also trying to understand your role in creating each of these. Many people with successful addiction recovery using the 12 Step program consider the self-discovery process that transpires between the sponsor and the sponsee in Steps 4 and 5 to be the single most important activity that takes place in the program.

Mindfulness, self-discovery, and integrity are brought together in Step 10 of the program. In Step 10, you are asked to practice all three on an ongoing basis. Step 10 involves learning to be aware (mindful), recognizing when you have had an unhealthy response to an event (real-time self-discovery), and taking immediate action to correct the situation (integrity). This action might be with another person, or it may be a situation where you have been treating yourself in an unhealthy way and need to take a new direction in your thinking regarding yourself.

Action Emphasis

The 12 Step program is an action-oriented approach to addressing addiction. This is an important feature that it shares with CBT for effecting change in thinking and behavior in a person. The action-emphasis of the 12 Step program, like CBT, is different than other approaches to personal transformation that are more focused on exploring the past and developing deep insight into the unconscious explanations for one's behavior.

The goal of both 12 Step recovery and CBT is for you to take your new perspective and tools and put these into practice. Without this, you will continue to "wallow" in the problem rather than living in the solution. The 12 Step program has a strong action orientation. Steps 6, 7, 8, 9, and 10 are all directives to take action toward "implementing" the new version of you. Combined with enhanced empowerment, integrity, and other improvements, developing an action emphasis is an essential element of your personal transformation.

Purposeful Repetition

Learning and retention of new skills require repetition. It is the only way that the changes from unhealthy thought processes to new proactive, supportive ones can be achieved. The need to repeat things to effect change is not speculation, it is fundamental to both the science and psychology of change. The ability of the brain to build new pathways for the storage and retrieval of healthy thoughts and behaviors is called neuroplasticity. It is the ability of the brain to "rewire" itself. Through repetition, healthy thinking and actions become the dominant process.

Most people suffering from addictive thinking have been stuck in a repetitive cycle of negative thoughts surrounding their addiction. Each repetition of the problem thinking, and related emotions and actions, strengthens the pathways to these thoughts in the brain. The brain is very efficient. It assumes that what you think about a lot is important to you, and it gives you easy access to it, making these thoughts more dominant in your thinking. The only way to change this cycle is through the purposeful repetition of new healthy thoughts and actions.

The 12 Step program, like CBT, is rich in practices for taking advantage of the neuroplasticity of the brain. First and foremost, the 12 Step program is not a one-time set of events that you "graduate" from when you have completed Step 12. It is a process that you build into your day-to-day life and reinforce through ongoing participation in the 12 Step program and mutual support network. Most people with successful recovery repeat working through the Steps periodically. Each time, they discover a deeper understanding of themselves and the tools of productive, healthy living offered by the 12 Step program.

Recommended Action Plan

The experience of participating in the 12 Step program of AA is normally much different and more rewarding than most people imagine. For some, the experience is like a spiritual awakening, others see it as a change in their fundamental character, and yet others view it as getting a new set of great tools to navigate life. It is not unusual for people participating in AA to express the wish that everyone in society had the opportunity to experience the personal change that the 12 Step process provides.

One of the hallmarks of the 12 Step program, and a major reason for its success, is that the basic action plan recommended to newcomers is very straightforward and uncomplicated. This basic plan has evolved over the decades and has been passed on by word of mouth to program participants. If you ask a person in AA today to suggest a plan of action, you will likely be told something like the following. This basic action plan is a solid starting point for 12 Step recovery.

The Basic Action Plan

- Abstain from using alcohol and drugs,
- Attend AA meetings on a regular basis,
- Read the Big Book of AA,
- Get a sponsor and work through the 12 Steps, and
- Participate in service work and helping others.

This straightforward set of goals is often characterized by AA participants as:

"A simple program for complicated people."

There are two good reasons for keeping the program of AA recovery straightforward and manageable for the newcomer. First, the person new to recovery is not usually in a good position emotionally and physically to take on a detailed, challenging set of tasks to remember and complete. Some AA participants might even advocate that the basic plan, described above, is still too much for the struggling newcomer to embrace and that, perhaps, something like: "Find an AA meeting and they will tell you what you need to do next" would suffice. We would be remiss if this were the only directive we gave you to start your 12 Step recovery program.

The second reason this basic plan of action has merit is that it provides a person the flexibility to augment the basic program with other recovery support that meets their personal needs. Many people start with the basic program and then use it as a foundation on which to build other activities that support the 12 Step process. These might include things like personal therapy, reading in the area of personal development, outdoor activities, and volunteer work.

The basic action plan is an excellent starting point for AA recovery, but your success will not be determined by your ability to check off the list of these basic program requirements as being "completed." Your success will ultimately be determined by the "quality" of your participation in the basic plan and what you do to build on it over time. As a result, the recommended plan of action advanced by *Modern 12 Step Recovery* includes a set of key success factors and potential roadblocks that you should use to guide your participation in the basic action plan.

Key Success Factors

In addition to taking the actions identified previously as the basic plan, a survey of people with more than ten years of successful recovery shows they would strongly recommend that you be guided along the way by the following key success factors. Understanding and embracing these can not be overemphasized.

Go All-In

A solid, personal commitment to the recovery process is the starting point for all effective recovery. Like the level of commitment required for recovery from any life-threatening illness, your commitment to the 12 Step program is not simply an acknowledgment of the need to "do something" about your problem. It is a serious, "all-in" dedication to the recovery process. If you are having doubts regarding your ability to make this commitment to your recovery, then you are setting yourself up for certain failure.

Keep It Real

Dishonesty is a way of life in addiction. It starts with the lies you tell yourself about the seriousness of your situation, including minimizing, rationalizing, projecting blame, and other self-deception. The dishonesty required to hide your use of alcohol and drugs can, alone, cause you to live a secret double life. For this reason, you must practice 100% honesty in your recovery program. Initially, most people entering recovery actually need to practice being honest because dishonesty is a tough habit to break. Without complete honesty with yourself and others, participating in a program based on sharing and self-discovery will fail.

Get Out of the Box

Those people who have success with recovery will approach it as a self-development, personal improvement endeavor. Those who take the approach that the 12 Step program is something being "done to you," something that you must endure, are misguided in their thinking.

Getting out of the box means looking at the entire recovery process with a sense of curiosity and humility, an opportunity to learn new things. Addiction recovery opens the door to a universe of self-actualization and an improved way of living. Reading materials outside of the AA literature in the areas of personal development and similar topics is common among people with successful recovery.

Be Patient

Alcohol and drugs were a "quick fix" approach to addressing your "stinking thinking." Recovery from addiction must be approached with patience and not being hard on yourself to fix the situation quickly. Some of the benefits, like not having to live a double life of deception, are realized quickly when you abstain from using. However, the real change occurs by systematically addressing all of the requirements of the basic program, while keeping the key success factors and potential roadblocks in mind.

Stay Focused

For the person new to recovery, paying attention can be a real challenge. Like being honest with yourself and others, staying focused (mindfulness) is something that you must practice. The thinking process of the person suffering from addiction is very internal and done in isolation. If you expect to gain new information and life skills you must—to put it very bluntly—pay attention. This includes being attentive to the new information being shared with you at AA meetings, in your reading, and in the other activities of the mutual support process. This improved focus also has significant rewards in your relationships with people outside of the program.

Keep Your Face Dry

Avoiding "wet faces and wet places," not hanging around settings where alcohol and drugs are being used, is some of the best advice on the planet. It is critical, particularly in the early stages of recovery, to keep yourself in recovery-friendly settings. You do not need to frequent bars with friends, attend weddings, go to private parties, or put yourself in any other situation where mind-altering substances are being used. Your self-importance will tell you that you need to participate: "What will they think of me?" The reality is that you are not that important—you do not need to compromise your sobriety.

Hang with the Winners

It is not enough to just avoid "wet faces and wet places." The people who experience long-term recovery make it a point to make connections with people in the recovery community. These are people who share something very personal with you, a common issue: your addiction. Introduce yourself and get contact information from several people who might share some things in common with you. To further support your recovery, be proactive about identifying someone with several years of recovery experience under their belt to be your sponsor. You do not need to be "buddies" with any of these people, although this does happen frequently.

Fill Up Your Toolkit

Many people in long-term recovery use other resources to complement and augment their basic AA action plan. This "Do whatever it takes!" approach to your recovery makes it interesting and improves your opportunity for success. These resources might include therapy with licensed psychiatrists or psychologists who specialize in addiction, reading literature on personal development topics, and meditation practice. The list of possible extracurricular activities is endless and fully supported by AA.

Go Fly a Kite

One of the best ways to augment your recovery activities in AA is to begin cultivating hobbies and activities that are interesting and engaging for you. Program participants take up a wide variety of new interests that take them outside of their addictive thinking and into healthy, rewarding experiences. Regular walking outdoors, crafts, volunteer work in the community, and other forms of hobbies are included in these activities.

Make it a Way of Life

The program should be viewed as a life-long commitment, a way of life, not something you "graduate" from after completing the basic plan and working the 12 Steps. Those people who experience successful, long-term recovery continue attending meetings and participating in the mutual support process on an ongoing basis because they enjoy it and it is essential to the maintenance of their recovery.

Be an AA Explorer

The book titled *Alcoholics Anonymous* ("the Big Book") is a historically significant, interesting document. The Big Book of AA introduced the longest-standing, most successful self-help program in history for addiction recovery. Regardless of your personal beliefs, religious or otherwise, keep an open mind. Read the Big Book and other major AA publications as great places to go exploring. Even people who come from a completely secular, non-religious position consider the Big Book an essential part of recovery in AA. That is why reading the Big Book is part of the basic action plan and is supported by *Modern 12 Step Recovery*.

Potential Roadblocks

If you are engaged in the basic action plan and being guided by the key success factors that were just described, your opportunity for success is excellent. There are, however, several possible obstacles that you might encounter that can be roadblocks to success. If you are struggling with one or more of these, you need to be diligent about recognizing it, getting assistance, and moving forward with determination.

Putting Your Head in the Sand

Despite all evidence to the contrary, you might still believe that you do not have an addiction issue. This denial is common in people because of the irrational thinking brought on by the addiction. The fortunate people recognize and accept that they have an addiction issue without anything disastrous occurring in their lives. Others are not so fortunate, relying on "wake-up calls" like a tragic car accident, financial ruin, or some other disruption in their lives to convince them that they are not well. If you have reached this point in the book and you still have doubts about having a substance-abuse problem, you should read the section in the Appendix titled *Are You Addicted?*

Using Alco-Logic

The strong physical and emotional desire to continue using, combined with the guilt and shame associated with the addiction, will cause you to rationalize your alcohol or drug use. These irrational explanations become things you begin to believe are facts or at least plausible reasons for your continued use of alcohol and drugs. As an example, one of the most common things you hear from people in early recovery is: "How am I going to function socially without being able to drink, when it is part of the activities of my work events and gatherings with my friends and family?" They say this with the conviction that life as they know it will end; there will be no more fun in life if they stop using alcohol and drugs. Some of the "alco-logic" used to rationalize addictive behavior by people is both creative and astounding!

Lowering the Bar

Another roadblock to success is minimizing the seriousness of the results of your addictive behavior. Drunk driving tickets, relationship issues, problems at work, and other consequences, things that would be considered serious issues to most people, are somehow minimized by addictive thinking. The person continues to "lower the bar" while awaiting something more severe. Unfortunately, killing a family while drunk driving, insanity, permanent wheelchair confinement, and death are all real possibilities for the individual who is not objective about what is going on.

Attempting "Magic" Tricks

The wish of all substance abusers is that they can somehow return to being a recreational user of mind-altering substances like other people they know. At some point, everyone with an addiction issue will make attempts to change their drinking or drug habits to convert themselves back to being a "normal user." Here is a paragraph from the Big Book of AA that describes attempts of the early AA participants to become "normal drinkers." It has a sense of irony and humor about it, but the participants in 1930s AA were deadly serious about the implications of living with this type of misguided thinking. The following description from the Big Book is still relevant today.

"Here are some of the methods we have tried: Drinking beer only, limiting the number of drinks, never drinking alone, never drinking in the morning, drinking only at home, never having it in the house, never drinking during business hours, drinking only at parties, switching from scotch to brandy, drinking only natural wines, agreeing to resign if ever drunk on the job, taking a trip, not taking a trip, swearing off forever (with and without a solemn oath), taking more physical exercise, reading inspirational books, going to health farms and sanitariums, accepting voluntary commitment to asylums. We could increase the list ad infinitum."

There is only one path back for the person with an addiction. It is total abstinence from mind-altering substances combined with a program of personal transformation.

Believing You Are "Special"

A critical error made by some people entering AA is thinking that they are somehow a "special case," not like all of the other "drunks" participating in the 12 Step program. Taking this view, they discount what is being shared by others at AA meetings and otherwise fight the process under the premise that their situation is different. There is a term for people who are like this; they are said to be "tragically unique."

Arrogance and Defiance

The biggest deterrent to success in the 12 Step program is behaving with an attitude of arrogance and defiance about your addiction. Quoting the AA founders from the Big Book:

"Those who do not recover are people who cannot or will not completely give themselves to this simple program, usually men and women who are constitutionally incapable of being honest with themselves."

Working Guide for the 12 Steps

This section provides a guide to learning and practicing the 12 Steps. For each Step, you are provided the following:

- The Step
- The single-word description
- An interpretation of the Step
- The psychology of the Step
- Several recommended actions
- Ideas for additional exercises
- Suggested reading topics

If you are interested in conducting a modern 12 Step recovery meeting, updated versions of selected AA readings that are used to open and close meetings are provided in the Appendix. Enjoy your journey in the 12 Step program. Welcome to AA!

Step 1

The Step

We admitted we were powerless over our addiction—that our lives had become unmanageable.

Single-Word Description

Acceptance

Interpretation

You accept that you have a physical and psychological illness that you cannot address by exercising willpower or by taking other misguided actions. The addictive thinking and behavior have created undesirable consequences in your life that are impacting your well-being and your relationships with the people, places, and things around you.

The Psychology of the Step

The use of mind-altering substances is an avoidance-based approach to addressing self-esteem and other issues. After prolonged use, the substance is also required to satisfy the physical addiction. Using this avoidance-based coping method produces unmanageable consequences. This approach must be abandoned and replaced with healthier ways of dealing with normal, day-to-day issues in your life.

Recommended Actions

- Discontinue the use of all mind-altering substances, permanently abstaining. Don't pick up the first one.

- Begin attending AA meetings today. Attend ninety meetings in the first ninety days and several per week going forward.

- Avoid "wet faces and wet places." (There are only rare events that you must attend. Do not be self-important. Your recovery is your #1 objective.)

Additional Exercises

- List the attempts you have made to moderate or completely quit your use of alcohol or drugs.

- Identify all of the consequences of your "stinking thinking" and substance abuse, including relationship problems, illness, missed opportunities, financial issues, embarrassing incidents, and other outcomes.

- Outline how your addiction has impacted your perception of yourself.

Suggested Reading Topics

Seek out information on the science and psychology behind addiction, including the impact on the brain, the body, and the changes in thinking and decision making that accompany addiction.

Steps 2 & 3

The Steps

2. Came to trust that resources outside of ourselves could restore us to rational thinking and behavior.

3. Made a decision to turn our direction and actions over to the guidance of those resources.

Single-Word Descriptions

Trust and Commitment

Interpretation

Considering your repeated, failed attempts to quit using alcohol and drugs, you have come to trust that using medical, psychological, and spiritual resources outside of you is critical (Step 2). Then, you surrender to the fact that you are incapable of addressing your addiction on your own and commit 100% to use those resources (Step 3).

The Psychology of the Step

The person who is addicted to alcohol and drugs is operating with a rigid set of beliefs and assumptions about both the addiction and the world around them. New information and actions, directed from outside of them, are needed or the situation will get progressively worse. To make this work, the person must be proactive about engaging these resources.

Recommended Actions

- After you have attended a few AA meetings, be assertive about identifying someone to be your sponsor. Find someone knowledgeable about the program who you feel comfortable with personally. Do not be concerned about asking people; they expect your request and want to help!

- Get the contact information for several people you encounter at meetings who have experience with recovery. Surrounding yourself with "the winners" improves your opportunity for success.

Additional Exercises

- Ask several experienced AA participants about the different types of physical, psychological, and spiritual support they use outside of the AA program.

- Engage your sponsor in a discussion about how a person's ego, self-image, and vanity can get in the way of them accepting addiction treatment, even when they have been presented with overwhelming evidence of their addiction.

Suggested Reading Topics

Look for articles on the role of acceptance and commitment in the recovery process, sources of denial, and the different types of support that people access for addiction recovery.

Step 4

The Step

Made an honest and thorough list of the issues in our lives.

Single-Word Description

Introspection

Interpretation

Step 4 is the first stage of the self-discovery process. It involves identifying, in writing, your resentments, fears, guilt, jealousy, and other issues impacting your life today. Central to this process is learning to understand your role in creating these issues in your life. Being completely honest and thorough about your work in this Step is integral to the process.

The Psychology of the Step

The starting point for developing more cognitive flexibility is to identify your problematic thoughts, emotions, and behaviors. This self-discovery is the foundation for exploring healthier alternatives. Taking responsibility for your emotions and actions is essential for moving you from being a person operating on self-deception to someone navigating life in a fact-based, flexible manner.

Recommended Actions

- Meet with your sponsor and review the Step 4 Process Guide in the Appendix. Establish a date for completing your Step 4 issues list.

- Using the Step 4 Process Guide, develop a list of the issues in your life and cultivate an understanding of your role in each of the issues.

- Be diligent about completing your Step 4 work by the date you agreed to while keeping in mind that it must be thorough and grounded in 100% honesty.

Additional Exercises

- Write down a list of all of your positive personal characteristics, things you like about yourself. You can use the list of positive character traits in the Appendix to help you with this self-exploration.

- Make a list of some of the people you admire and write down what you admire about them. These people could be friends, family members, or public figures.

Suggested Reading Topics

Explore books and articles on the subjects of self-discovery, sources of resentments and fear, and the benefits of writing things down as a way of gaining personal insight.

Step 5

The Step

Admitted to ourselves and another person our specific role in those issues.

Single-Word Description

Affirmation

Interpretation

Step 5 is the second part of the self-discovery process you started in Step 4. The first part of Step 5 is having an honest dialogue with yourself about the areas you identified on your list, your role in these, and the changes you need to make in your thinking and actions. The second part of Step 5 is having an open and candid conversation with your sponsor about your issues and, again, your role in each of these.

The Psychology of the Step

Self-discovery and sharing those things in your life that create emotional and behavioral issues for you are at the center of modern psychology. Honesty with yourself is the starting point. Then, candid dialogue with your sponsor, similar to the confidential discussions you might have with a therapist in psychology, is a critical part of the self-discovery process in AA.

Recommended Actions

- Take your Step 4 list and read it as if you are an unrelated third-party reading about you. What actions would you recommend to this person (you) regarding changes they should consider in their thinking and behavior?

- Next, meet with your sponsor and review your Step 4 list. An open, candid, and honest dialogue is essential.

- Last, with your sponsor, take a "big picture" view of your Step 4 content. Look for areas that you can target for thinking and behavior changes in the future. If you have repeating negative character traits and cognitive distortions, these should be a priority.

Additional Exercises

- Based on what you have learned about yourself in Steps 4 and 5, consider the people you have relationships with and see if you can look at them with more compassion and empathy. They all have challenges in their lives.

- Use your complaints about other people as a way to further your understanding of yourself.

Suggested Reading Topics

There are numerous articles available on the benefits of open and honest sharing of your problems with another person. Information on the importance of the sponsor/sponsee relationship in AA is also enlightening.

Steps 6 and 7

The Steps

6. Became entirely ready to make changes in our character.

7. Began making changes in our thinking and behavior with humility and honesty.

Single-Word Descriptions

Determination and Transformation

Interpretation

The first of these, Step 6, is the important action you take to empower yourself to change. This is a commitment to transform the way you view yourself and your interactions with the people, places, and things around you. This change is based on the guidance you received from your resources in Steps 2 and 3, and what you learned in the Step 4 and 5 self-discovery process. Step 7 is taking the critical action of going out into the world and gradually implementing the new version of yourself in everything you do.

The Psychology of the Step

Contemporary psychological therapy is action-oriented. Changing unhealthy thinking and behavior is not possible without setting goals and practicing the new skills.

Recommended Actions

- Using the information from Steps 4 and 5, develop a specific list of changes that you are going to focus on in the future. This should include, initially, a minimum of five positive character traits that you are going to practice in your interactions with yourself and others.

- Review the list of Cognitive Distortions periodically and make it a practice to recognize when you are making these "thinking errors."

- Start making the changes in your thinking and behavior today! Being the "new you" will take practice. There will be some trial and error involved, but you will be amazed at what even small changes can accomplish.

Additional Exercises

- Write down each of your negative character traits and cognitive distortions on a piece of paper. Then, say goodbye to these and shred the piece of paper.

- With your sponsor or another person in the program, invent a few typical relationship scenarios, and try role-playing several negative and positive character traits.

Suggested Reading Topics

Look for articles and books on personal change and techniques for making self-improvements.

Steps 8 and 9

The Steps

8. Made a list of all persons we had harmed and became willing to make amends to them all.

9. Made direct amends to those people wherever possible, except when to do so would injure them or others.

Single-Word Descriptions

Compassion and Reparation

Interpretation

In Step 8, you are making a list of the people you have impacted. These past indiscretions might include physical, emotional, financial, or other wrongdoings on your part. In Step 9, you will meet with these people to apologize for your behavior, make restitution, and inform them about your program of recovery. The potential for causing further harm to the person or others is a consideration in Step 9.

The Psychology of the Step

The honesty and compassion that come with Steps 8 and 9 are critical elements of a person's transformation. Taking responsibility for your past actions facilitates personal empowerment, which leads to replacing a blame-based model of living with a healthy, self-directed alternative.

Recommended Actions

- Obtain several Step 8 worksheet alternatives from the internet to consider.

- Engage your sponsor for assistance and guidance with the Step 8 worksheet and other aspects of Steps 8 and 9.

- Using your Step 4 list and the information from your Step 5 discussions, develop the Step 8 list of people with whom you need to make amends. Establish a specific time for completing the list.

- Review the completed list of potential amends with your sponsor and develop a plan and timeframe for each; then begin making the amends.

Additional Exercises

- There are situations where you may have been unfair to yourself. Investigate why putting yourself on the amends list can be an important aspect of Steps 8 and 9.

- Do trial runs of several of the amends with your sponsor, concentrating on different types (physical, emotional, financial, or some other form).

Suggested Reading Topics

The power of making restitution/amends as an avenue to personal growth is an interesting area to explore.

Step 10

The Step

Continued to be aware of our thoughts and actions, and when we are wrong promptly admitted it.

Single-Word Description

Diligence

Interpretation

Step 10 asks you to develop a practice of ongoing awareness regarding how you interpret events in your life and how you respond to these. If you become aware that your thoughts or actions are not consistent with the new principles of living that you are trying to cultivate, Step 10 recommends that you take timely action to remedy things. Call this making "real-time" amends if you like. The goal of Step 10, is to "keep your side of the street clean."

The Psychology of the Step

Developing the ability to have "real-time" awareness of your thoughts and actions is the foundation that Cognitive-Behavioral Therapy (CBT) is built on. In the ideal CBT scenario, you learn to pause, consider alternatives, and then choose the best alternative, rather than "shooting from the hip" and having to rectify the situation with hindsight.

Recommended Actions

- Begin, immediately, paying more attention to your surroundings and making it a practice to be focused and listen attentively to others in conversations.

- Don't respond to external events or internal thoughts with your first impulse action. Allow yourself the benefit of considering alternative interpretations of events and different ways of responding before you act.

- If you respond to a situation impulsively and discover later that there was a better alternative, correct the situation immediately.

Additional Exercises

- At your AA meetings, make it a point to listen attentively to what everyone is saying. If you "drift," pull yourself back.

- Before you go into situations, consider your expectations. Make certain that your motives are not self-serving, motives that will lead to actions that will require "mopping up" later.

Suggested Reading Topics

Read several articles on the art of listening, how to develop awareness, how to use the "Pause Button," and the ways you can be kind and loving to others.

Step 11

The Step

Pursued a program of ongoing self-improvement and empowerment through meditation, reflection, and study.

Single-Word Description

Evolution

Interpretation

Long-term success with your recovery is dependent on continuous improvement of your recovery skills and enhancing your ability to be self-directed. This includes reinforcement and refinement of your understanding of the 12 Step principles and seeking additional information from your other recovery resources (medical, psychological, and spiritual). As Step 11 suggests, there are several ways to approach this ongoing self-improvement and empowerment, including meditation, reflection, and further study.

The Psychology of the Step

Repetition and reinforcement of newly acquired skills and the pursuit of new information are all critical aspects of rewiring the brain and refreshing the executive function in the thinking process.

Recommended Actions

- Meet with your sponsor and complete a review of Steps 1 through 10, focusing on what you have learned to date.

- Ask your sponsor and several other AA contacts about books, articles, and podcasts that they would recommend to support your continued personal development.

- Take a class in meditation, one that provides a background in several of the meditation techniques.

Additional Exercises

- Make a list of things you can do, that are not 12 Step program-related, that will help you reinforce the AA principles.

- Consider changes you could begin making in your physical exercise and nutrition to support these important dimensions of recovery.

- Write down your definition of personal empowerment. Then, look up the definition using several sources and contrast it with your definition.

Suggested Reading Topics

Look for books and articles on medical, psychological, and spiritual guidance for recovery. Seek out several articles about how to become an empowered, self-directed person.

Step 12

The Step

Having experienced a personal transformation as a result of these steps, we tried to carry this program to other addicts and to practice these principles in all aspects of our lives.

Single-Word Description

Integration

Interpretation

Step 12 contains two very important recommendations that are gateways to successful long-term recovery. The first, and one of the principal discoveries of Bill Wilson and his "team" in the 1930s, is that helping others who are struggling with addiction is one of the best ways to help yourself. Helping others facilitates moving you from being a self-centered, addictive thinker to an "other-focused," compassionate person. The second recommendation in this Step is that the Steps are more than just a state of mind: they must be used in all aspects of everything you do in your life.

The Psychology of the Step

Central to all physiological and psychological change is reinforcement and practice of new, healthy skills. This Step provides directives for two of the most powerful ways of strengthening and maintaining your new state.

Recommended Actions

- Make sure that you are actively participating during your AA meetings. Stay focused on the specific Step or topic of discussion. Share your experience, strength, and hope with the group around the topic.

- After you have one or more years of sobriety, identify a newcomer to sponsor. Work with your sponsor and others in AA to establish effective guidelines for sponsorship.

- Go out into the world every day with solid intent and make a conscious effort to take the right actions.

Additional Exercises

- Meet with your sponsor and review how you are implementing the Steps and the principles of AA in your daily activities.

- Make sure to thank your sponsor for all of their support during the 12 Step process. Then, give yourself some credit for your progress—remembering that it is progress, not perfection, that is our goal!

Suggested Reading Topics

There is excellent material available on the benefits of helping others as an avenue to your own personal growth.

It works if you work it!

Anonymous

Appendix

Section	Page
• Are You Addicted?	94
• 12 Steps – Traditional	97
• The Doctor's Opinion	98
• Step 4 Process Guide	106
• Character Traits	111
• Cognitive Distortions	112
• Meeting Readings *	
o Serenity Statement	113
o Meeting Preamble	114
o The Promises	115
o How It Works	116
o More About Addiction	120
o Acceptance	123

* These are standard readings used to open and close AA meetings. There have been minor edits to these to make these compatible with the Modern 12 Steps.

Are You Addicted?

If you turn to the people in AA who are experiencing successful recovery and ask them to help you determine if you have an alcohol or drug problem, they will likely ask you to answer one simple question:

"<u>Are you continuing to use alcohol or drugs despite experiencing consequences from your ongoing use</u>?"

If your answer is "Yes" to this question, they would tell you that there is a high probability that you have an addiction issue. Many people in successful recovery would go as far as to say that the simple fact that you are concerned about being addicted and reading this book is adequate proof that you have an addiction issue present.

If you need to explore the subject further, there are several effective addiction assessment tools available online, through addiction treatment centers, and from therapists in private practice. Here is an example of an alcohol addiction assessment questionnaire adapted from the diagnostic criteria of the American Psychiatric Association (APA). This would also apply to drug addiction.

Keep in mind that any tool like this is only effective if you maintain a high level of integrity regarding being honest about your responses.

Alcohol Use Disorder
American Psychiatric Association (APA)

(Yes or No answer)

1. Alcohol is often taken in larger amounts or over longer periods than intended.

2. There have been unsuccessful efforts to cut down or control the use of alcohol.

3. A great deal of time is spent in activities necessary to obtain alcohol, use alcohol, or recover from its effects.

4. The strong desire or urge to use alcohol (craving) is present.

5. Alcohol use is resulting in a failure to fulfill major obligations at work, school, or home.

6. The use of alcohol is continued despite having persistent social or interpersonal problems.

7. Important social, occupational, or recreational activities have been completely given up or reduced because of alcohol use.

8. Alcohol is being used in situations that could be physically hazardous, including driving and other situations.

9. There is continued use of alcohol despite persistent physical or psychological problems caused by it.

10. An increase in tolerance is being experienced. More is needed to achieve the desired effect.

11. Withdrawal is being experienced in the form of one or more physical or psychological symptoms when you discontinue use (e.g., vomiting, sweating, tremors, insomnia, nausea, or anxiety).

The APA would suggest that if you answer Yes to 2-3 of these, there is alcohol abuse disorder present; 4-5, and the disorder is elevated; more than 5, the condition is severe. Experience in the mutual support network of AA shows that if you have even a couple of these behaviors present in your life, you should be concerned.

The 12 Steps - Traditional

1. We admitted we were powerless over alcohol—that our lives had become unmanageable.

2. Came to believe that a Power greater than ourselves could restore us to sanity.

3. Made a decision to turn our will and our lives over to the care of God as we understood Him.

4. Made a searching and fearless moral inventory of ourselves.

5. Admitted to God, to ourselves, and to another human being the exact nature of our wrongs.

6. Were entirely ready to have God remove all these defects of character.

7. Humbly asked Him to remove our shortcomings.

8. Made a list of all persons we had harmed, and became willing to make amends to them all.

9. Made direct amends to such people wherever possible, except when to do so would injure them or others.

10. Continued to take personal inventory and when we were wrong promptly admitted it.

11. Sought through prayer and meditation to improve our conscious contact with God as we understood Him, praying only for knowledge of His will for us and the power to carry that out.

12. Having had a spiritual awakening as the result of these steps, we tried to carry this message to alcoholics, and to practice these principles in all our affairs.

The Doctor's Opinion
Alcoholics Anonymous - "The Big Book"
(Excerpts from Dr. Silkworth's historical letters.)

Dr. Silkworth writes (1939):

The subject presented in this book **[Note: The Big Book]** seems to me to be of paramount importance to those afflicted with alcoholic addiction.

I say this after many years' experience as Medical Director of one of the oldest hospitals in the country treating alcoholic and drug addiction.

There was, therefore, a sense of real satisfaction when I was asked to contribute a few words on a subject which is covered in such masterly detail in these pages.

We doctors have realized for a long time that some form of moral psychology was of urgent importance to alcoholics, but its application presented difficulties beyond our conception. What with our ultra-modern standards, our scientific approach to everything, we are perhaps not well equipped to apply the powers of good that lie outside our synthetic knowledge.

Many years ago one of the leading contributors to this book came under our care in this hospital and while here he **[Note:**

Bill Wilson] acquired some ideas which he put into practical application at once.

Later, he requested the privilege of being allowed to tell his story to other patients here, and with some misgiving, we consented. The cases we have followed through have been most interesting: in fact, many of them are amazing. The unselfishness of these men as we have come to know them, the entire absence of profit motive, and their community spirit, is indeed inspiring to one who has labored long and wearily in this alcoholic field. They believe in themselves, and still more in the power which pulls chronic alcoholics back from the gates of death.

Of course, an alcoholic ought to be freed from his physical craving for liquor, and this often requires a definite hospital procedure, before psychological measures can be of maximum benefit.

We believe, and so suggested a few years ago, that the action of alcohol on these chronic alcoholics is a manifestation of an allergy **[Note: The genetic predisposition]**; that the phenomenon of craving is limited to this class and never occurs in the average temperate drinker. These allergic types can never safely use alcohol in any form at all; and once having formed the habit and found they cannot break it, once having lost their self-confidence, their reliance upon things human, their problems pile up on them and become astonishingly difficult to solve.

Frothy emotional appeal seldom suffices. The message which can interest and hold these alcoholic people must have depth and weight. In nearly all cases, their ideals must be grounded in a power outside of themselves, if they are to re-create their lives.

If any feel that as psychiatrists directing a hospital for alcoholics we appear somewhat sentimental, let them stand with us a while on the firing line, see the tragedies, the despairing wives, the little children; let the solving of these problems become a part of their daily work, and even of their sleeping moments, and the most cynical will not wonder that we have accepted and encouraged this movement. We feel, after many years of experience, that we have found nothing which has contributed more to the rehabilitation of these men than the altruistic movement now growing up among them **[Note: Alcoholics Anonymous]**.

Men and women drink essentially because they like the effect produced by alcohol. The sensation is so elusive that, while they admit it is injurious, they cannot after a time differentiate the true from the false. To them, their alcoholic life seems the only normal one. They are restless, irritable, and discontented unless they can again experience the sense of ease and comfort which comes at once by taking a few drinks—drinks which they see others taking with impunity. After they have succumbed to the desire again, as so many do, and the phenomenon of craving develops, they pass through the well-known stages of a spree, emerging remorseful, with a firm resolution not to drink again. This is repeated over and over, and unless this person can experience an entire psychic change there is very little hope of his recovery.

On the other hand—and strange as this may seem to those who do not understand—once a psychic change has occurred, the very same person who seemed doomed, who had so many problems he despaired of ever solving them, suddenly finds himself easily able to control his desire for alcohol, the only effort necessary being that required to follow a few simple rules **[Note: The Steps]**.

Men have cried out to me in sincere and despairing appeal: "Doctor, I cannot go on like this! I have everything to live for! I must stop, but I cannot! You must help me!"

Faced with this problem, if a doctor is honest with himself, he must sometimes feel his own inadequacy. Although he gives all that is in him, it often is not enough. One feels that something more than their power is needed to produce the essential psychic change. Though the aggregate of recoveries resulting from psychiatric effort is considerable, we physicians must admit we have made little impression upon the problem as a whole. Many types do not respond to the ordinary psychological approach.

I do not hold with those who believe that alcoholism is entirely a problem of mental control. I have had many men who had, for example, worked a period of months on some problem or business deal which was to be settled on a certain date, favorably to them. They took a drink a day or so prior to the date, and then the phenomenon of craving at once became paramount to all other interests so that the important appointment was not met. These men were not drinking to escape; they were drinking to overcome a craving beyond their mental control.

There are many situations that arise out of the phenomenon of craving which cause men to make the supreme sacrifice rather then continue to fight.

The classification of alcoholics seems most difficult, and in much detail is outside the scope of this book. There are, of course, psychopaths who are emotionally unstable. We are all familiar with this type. They are always "going on the wagon for keeps." They are over-remorseful and make many resolutions, but never a decision.

There is the type of man who is unwilling to admit that he cannot take a drink. He plans various ways of drinking. He changes his brand or his environment. There is the type who always believes that after being entirely free from alcohol for a period of time he can take a drink without danger. There is the manic-depressive type, who is, perhaps, the least understood by his friends, and about whom a whole chapter could be written.

Then there are types entirely normal in every respect except in the effect alcohol has upon them. They are often able, intelligent, friendly people.

All these, and many others, have one symptom in common: they cannot start drinking without developing the phenomenon of craving. This phenomenon, as we have suggested, may be the manifestation of an allergy that differentiates these people, and sets them apart as a distinct entity. It has never been, by any treatment with which we are familiar, permanently eradicated. The only relief we have to suggest is entire abstinence.

This immediately precipitates us into a seething cauldron of debate. Much has been written pro and con, but among physicians, the general opinion seems to be that most chronic alcoholics are doomed. What is the solution? Perhaps I can best answer this by relating one of my experiences.

About one year prior to this experience a man was brought in to be treated for chronic alcoholism. He had but partially recovered from a gastric hemorrhage and seemed to a case of pathological mental deterioration. He has lost everything worthwhile in life and was only living, one might say, to drink. He frankly admitted and believed that for him there was no hope. Following the elimination of alcohol, there was found to be no permanent brain injury. He accepted the plan outlined in this book. One year later he called to see me, and I experienced a very strange sensation. I knew the man by name, and partly recognized his features, but there all resemblance ended. From a trembling, despairing, nervous wreck, had emerged a man brimming over with self-reliance and contentment. I talked with him for some time, but was not able to bring myself to feel that I had known him before. To me, he was a stranger, and so he left me. A long time has passed with no return to alcohol.

When I need a mental uplift, I often think of another case brought in by a physician prominent in New York. The patient had made his own diagnosis and deciding his situation hopeless, had hidden in a deserted barn determined to die. He was rescued by a searching party, and, in desperate condition, brought to me. Following his physical rehabilitation, he had a talk with me in which he frankly stated he thought the treatment a waste of effort, unless I could assure him, which no one ever had, that in the future he would have the "will power" to resist the impulse to drink.

His alcoholic problem was so complex and his depression so great, that we felt his only hope would be through what we then called "moral psychology," and we doubted if even that would have any effect.

However, he did become "sold" on the ideas contained in this book. He has not had a drink for a great many years. I see him now and then and he is as fine a specimen of manhood as one could wish to meet.

I earnestly advise every alcoholic to read this book through, and though perhaps he came to scoff, he may remain to pray.

Modern 12 Step Recovery
Step 4 Process Guide

Introduction

This guide is a suggested process for completing your Step 4 issues list. The role of Step 4 is to accomplish two important goals:

- Get all of the issues in your life "out on the table," and
- Take an objective look at each issue and gain insight into what your role was in contributing to it.

The information from Step 4 is used as the basis for determining changes in your thinking and behavior in Steps 5, 6, and 7.

This suggested Step 4 process is very straightforward. The key to it is being thorough and honest. Read this short process guide entirely, studying the examples along the way, before you start developing your list of issues.

Part I - Identification of the Issues in Your Life

The first part of the process is to "brainstorm" a list of the issues that you presently have in your life. This can be anything that comes to mind, past, present, or future, <u>that impacts you today</u>. The goal is to not "get into the weeds" with details. Just get these down on paper.

Use the following table to help you recall and describe your issues. For each issue, write a short, one or two sentence, description. In that description, make sure to specifically identify **How** you feel, **Who** your feeling is directed toward, and **How** you are impacted. Three examples follow the tables.

Table I - HOW do you feel?			
Resentful	Fearful	Betrayed	Controlled
Deceived	Guilty	Insecure	Jealous
Lonely	Manipulated	Powerless	Sad

Table II - WHO is the feeling about?			
Individuals	Parent	Partner	Ex-Partner
Sibling	Relative	Friend	Co-Worker
Teacher	Stranger	Clergyman	Yourself
Institutions	Government	Legal System	Education
Employer	Business	Religion	Health System
Races/Cultures	Politics	Marriage	Jails/Prisons

Table III - WHAT is the impact on you?			
Physical	Sexual	Emotional	Money
Material Items	Appearance	Career	Social Status
Partner Status	Freedom	Self-image	Confidence

Examples of Issues

1. **Issue:** I **resent** my **sister and her husband**. I loaned them $1,000 ten years ago from **savings**. They never paid me back.

2. **Issue:** I am **lonely**. My last two **girlfriends** left me. My **self-confidence** is shot. I am a great guy, with a nice car, apartment, and a good job. The guys they are dating now are real losers. I don't get it.

3. **Issue:** I am living with a lot of **fear** of the **legal system**. If I get another DUI (Driving Under the Influence citation) I am going to lose my **freedom** and go to jail.

Part II - Identification of Your Role in the Issues

After completing your list of issues, the next step in the process is to take an objective, honest look at how you might have contributed to creating each issue and/or perpetuating it. You will find this self-discovery very interesting and informative, as it provides perspective on each issue that you might have not considered.

There are two activities in Part II. First, you will take a look at a list of character traits (personality characteristics) that you could have brought to the issue. Second, you will be reviewing a list of potential cognitive distortions ("thinking errors") that may have been involved in your decision making.

For each issue on your list, complete the following:

1. **Character Traits** – Carefully review the negative character traits on page 111. Identify one or more of these traits from the list that you may have brought to the issue.

2. **Cognitive Distortions ("Thinking Errors")** – Carefully examine the list of cognitive distortions on page 112. Determine if you might have one or more of these "thinking errors" involved in this issue.

Following are the example issues from earlier, updated for character traits and cognitive distortions that the person brought to each issue.

Issue Examples – Updated for Self-Discovery

1. **Issue: I resent my sister and her husband.** I loaned them $1,000 ten years ago from my **savings**. They never paid me back. **Self-discovery:** Perhaps I was being impractical. My sister and her husband were unemployed when I loaned them the money and they have not worked for most of the past ten years. There was a good chance they were not going to pay me back **(trait – unrealistic)**. Also, I am looking at this from the worst possible perspective **(distortion – catastrophizing)**. We have a great

relationship otherwise. If they never pay me back, I am OK financially.

2. **Issue:** I am **lonely**. My last two **girlfriends** left me. My **self-confidence** is shot. I am a great guy, with a nice car, apartment, and a good job. The guys they are dating now are real losers. I don't get it. **Self-discovery:** Their new boyfriends do not have any of the nice things I have. Perhaps my ex-girlfriends are not impressed by what I own **(trait – materialistic).** Further, it is not rational for me to think that I am going to be alone forever **(distortion – all-or-nothing thinking).** Perhaps I need to be more kind and loving.

3. **Issue:** I am living with a lot of **fear** of the **legal system.** If I get another DUI, I am going to lose my **freedom** and go to jail. **Self-discovery:** I am not active in a program of addiction recovery like they recommended **(traits – procrastinating and undisciplined).** I am not a loser in general **(distortion – overgeneralization).** I am an alcoholic.

You can write all of this information down in any format you choose. What is important is that you have an accurate description (Part I) and that you have documented any of your character traits and cognitive distortions (Part II). After you have completed Part I and II for each issue, meet with your sponsor on Step 5.

Character Traits

Negative	Positive	Negative	Positive
Aggressive	Gentle	Judgmental	Accepting
Angry	Content	Lazy	Industrious
Apathetic	Interested	Manipulative	Collaborative
Arrogant	Humble	Materialistic	Spiritual
Boastful	Modest	Emotional	Level-headed
Conceited	Humble	Perfectionist	Realistic
Controlling	Sharing	Possessive	Generous
Cowardly	Brave	Prejudiced	Open-minded
Critical	Non-judging	Procrastinating	Action-based
Cynical	Optimistic	Resist change	Flexible
Defensive	Open	Rude	Courteous
Dishonest	Honest	Self-important	Humble
Disrespectful	Reverent	Self-centered	Caring
Envying	Confident	Self-pitying	Grateful
Exaggerating	Modest	Shy	Outgoing
Greedy	Generous	Spiteful	Loving
Hateful	Forgiving	Superior	Humble
Hypersensitive	Tolerant	Suspicious	Trusting
Ill-tempered	Good-natured	Undisciplined	Organized
Impatient	Tolerant	Unrealistic	Practical
Impulsive	Disciplined	Untrustworthy	Reliable
Inconsiderate	Thoughtful	Vain	Modest
Indecisive	Resolute	Vindictive	Forgiving
Inflexible	Open-minded	Violent	Gentle
Insecure	Self-confident	Vulgar	Polite
Intolerant	Patient	Wasteful	Thrifty
Irresponsible	Reliable	Verbose	Succinct

Cognitive Distortions *
("Thinking Errors")

1. **All-Or-Nothing Thinking** – Thinking in extremes; no room for grey areas.

2. **Overgeneralization** – Based on a single occurrence, you conclude that it will continue to repeat.

3. **Mental Filtering** – Focusing only on the negative aspects of things and ignoring the positive.

4. **Disqualifying the Positive** – Discounting positive experiences. They do not count for one reason or another.

5. **Mind Reading / Fortune Telling** – Jumping to the conclusion that the outcome will be negative without supporting facts.

6. **Catastrophizing (Magnification)** – Dwelling on the worst- or best-case scenario occurring due to a single event.

7. **Emotional Reasoning** – Believing that if I feel this way, it must be true.

8. **Shoulds** – Self-defeating ways we attempt to motivate ourselves and others with unrealistic expectations, only to ultimately feel a failure when these are not met.

9. **Labeling** – Extreme generalization. I am a loser versus I made a mistake.

10. **Personalization and Blame** – Blaming yourself or others for situations that were not directly under your control.

* These are ten "errors" in thinking that contribute to problems that people have in their lives. These were identified by Dr. Aaron T. Beck and expanded on by Dr. David D. Burns in their groundbreaking work in Cognitive Behavioral Therapy (CBT).

Serenity Statement

Grant me the serenity:

To accept the things I cannot change,

The courage to change the things I can, and

The wisdom to know the difference.

Meeting Preamble

Alcoholics Anonymous is a mutual support network of men and women who share their experience, strength, and hope with each other that they may solve their common problem and help others to recover from alcoholism. The only requirement for membership is a desire to stop drinking. There are no dues or fees for AA membership; we are self-supporting through our own contributions. AA is not allied with any sect, denomination, politics, organization, or institution; does not wish to engage in any controversy, neither endorses nor opposes any causes. Our primary purpose is to stay sober and help other alcoholics to achieve sobriety.

The Promises

If we are painstaking about this phase of our development, we will be amazed before we are halfway through. We are going to know a new freedom and a new happiness. We will not regret the past nor wish to shut the door on it. We will comprehend the word serenity and we will know peace. No matter how far down the scale we have gone, we will see how our experience can benefit others. That feeling of uselessness and self-pity will disappear. We will lose interest in selfish things and gain interest in our fellows. Self-seeking will slip away. Our whole attitude and outlook on life will change. Fear of people and economic insecurity will leave us. We will intuitively know how to handle situations which used to baffle us. We will suddenly realize that our external resources are doing for us what we could not do for ourselves. Are these extravagant promises? We think not. They are being fulfilled among us – sometimes quickly, sometimes slowly. They will always materialize if we work for them.

How It Works

Rarely have we seen a person fail who has thoroughly followed our path. Those who do not recover are people who cannot or will not completely give themselves to this simple program, usually men and women who are constitutionally incapable of being honest with themselves. There are such unfortunates. They are not at fault; they seem to have been born that way. They are naturally incapable of grasping and developing a manner of living which demands rigorous honesty. Their chances are less than average. There are those, too, who suffer from grave emotional and mental disorders, but many of them do recover if they have the capacity to be honest.

Our stories disclose in a general way what we used to be like, what happened, and what we are like now. If you have decided you want what we have and are willing to go to any length to get it – then you are ready to take certain steps.

At some of these we balked. We thought we could find an easier, softer way. But we could not. With all the earnestness at our command, we beg of you to be fearless and thorough from the very start. Some of us have tried to hold on to our old ideas and the result was nil until we let go absolutely.

Remember that we deal with alcohol – cunning, baffling, and powerful! Without help it is too much for us. But there are external resources available. May you find these now!

Half measures availed us nothing. We stood at the turning point. We asked for inspiration and guidance with complete abandon.

Here are the Steps we took, which are suggested as a program of recovery:

1. We admitted we were powerless over our addiction–that our lives had become unmanageable.

2. Came to trust that resources outside of ourselves could restore us to rational thinking and behavior.

3. Made a decision to turn our direction and actions over to the guidance of those

resources.

4. Made an honest and thorough list of the issues in our lives.

5. Admitted to ourselves and another person our specific role in those issues.

6. Became entirely ready to make changes in our character.

7. Began making changes in our thinking and behavior with humility and honesty.

8. Made a list of all persons we had harmed and became willing to make amends to them all.

9. Made direct amends to those people wherever possible, except when to do so would injure them or others.

10. Continued to be aware of our thoughts and actions and when we were wrong promptly admitted it.

11. Pursued a program of ongoing self-improvement and empowerment through meditation, reflection, and study.

12. Having experienced a personal transformation as a result of these steps, we tried to carry this

program to other addicts and to practice these principles in all aspects of our lives.

Many of us exclaimed, "What an order! I can't go through with it." Do not be discouraged. No one among us has been able to maintain anything like perfect adherence to these principles. We are not saints. The point is, that we are willing to grow along spiritual lines. The principles we have set down are guides to progress. We claim spiritual progress rather than spiritual perfection.

Our description of the alcoholic, the chapter to the agnostic, and our personal adventures before and after make clear three pertinent ideas:

(a) That we were alcoholic and could not manage our own lives.
(b) That outside support would be required to relieve our alcoholism.
(c) That these resources would help us if we sought these out.

More About Alcoholism

Most of us have been unwilling to admit we were real alcoholics. No person likes to think that they are bodily and mentally different than others. Therefore, it is not surprising that our drinking careers have been characterized by countless vain attempts to prove we could drink like other people. The idea that somehow, someday you will control and enjoy your drinking is the great obsession of every abnormal drinker. The persistence of this illusion is astonishing. Many pursue it into the gates of insanity or death.

We learned that we had to fully concede to our innermost selves that we were alcoholics. This is the first step in recovery. The delusion that we are like other people, or presently may be, has to be smashed.

We alcoholics are men and women who have lost the ability to control our drinking. We know that no real alcoholic ever recovers control. All of us felt at times that we were regaining control, but such intervals—usually brief—were inevitably followed by still less control, which led in time to pitiful and incomprehensible demoralization. We are convinced to a person that alcoholics of our type are in the grip of a progressive illness. Over any considerable period, we get worse, never better.

We are like people who have lost their legs; they never grow new ones. Neither does there appear to be any kind of treatment that will make alcoholics of our kind like other people. We have tried every imaginable remedy. In some instances, there has been brief recovery, followed always by a still worse relapse. Physicians who are familiar with alcoholism agree there is no such thing as making a normal drinker out of an alcoholic. Science may one day accomplish this, but it hasn't done so yet.

Despite all we can say, many who are real alcoholics are not going to believe they are in that class. By every form of self-deception and experimentation, they will try to prove themselves exceptions to the rule, therefore nonalcoholic. If anyone who is showing an inability to control his drinking can do the right-about-face and drink like a gentleman, our hats are off to him. Heaven knows, we have tried hard enough and long enough to drink like other people!

Here are some of the methods we have tried: Drinking beer only, limiting the number of drinks, never drinking alone, never drinking in the morning, drinking only at home, never having it in the house, never drinking during business hours, drinking only at parties, switching from scotch to brandy, drinking only natural wines, agreeing to resign if ever drunk on the job, taking a trip, not taking a trip, swearing off forever (with and without a solemn oath), taking more physical exercise, reading inspirational books, going to health farms and sanitariums, accepting voluntary commitment to asylums – we could increase the list ad infinitum.

Acceptance

Acceptance is the answer to all my problems today. When I am disturbed, it is because I find some person, place, thing, or situation – some fact of my life – unacceptable to me. I can find no serenity until I accept that person, place, thing, or situation as being exactly as it is at this moment. Until I could accept my alcoholism, I could not stay sober; unless I accept life completely on life's terms, I cannot be happy. I need to concentrate not so much on what needs to be changed in the world as on what needs to be changed in me and my attitudes.

Bibliography

B., Dick – The Oxford Group & Alcoholics Anonymous: A Design for Living that Works – Paradise Research Publications – 2008

Beck, Aaron T., M.D. – Cognitive Therapy and the Emotional Disorders – Penguin Group – 1979

Beck, Judith S. – Cognitive Behavioral Therapy – Basics and Beyond – The Guilford Press – 2011

Berger, Allen, Ph.D. – 12 Smart Things to Do When the Booze and Drugs Are Gone – Hazelden Publishing – 2010

Branch, Rhena and Wilson, Rob – Cognitive Behavioural Therapy for Dummies – John Wiley and Sons – 2010

Burns, David D., M.D. – Feeling Good – The New Mood Therapy – William Morrow and Company – 1980

Cheever, Susan – My Name Is Bill – His Life and Creation of Alcoholics Anonymous – Washington Square Press – 2004

Cheever, Susan – Time 100: Bill Wilson – Time Magazine – 1999

Edwards, Griffith – Alcohol: The World's Favorite Drug – Thomas Dunne Books – 2002

Ellis, Albert and Harper, Robert A. and Powers, Melvin – A Guide to Rational Living – Wilshire Book Company – 1975

Bibliography
(Continued)

General Services Office – Alcoholics Anonymous – Membership and Other Statistics – 2019

Gorski, Terrence T. and Miller, Merlene – Staying Sober – Independence Press – 1986

James, William – The Varieties of Religious Experiences: A Study in Human Nature – Seven Treasures Publications – 1902

Ketcham, Katherine and Milam, James Robert – Under the Influence – Bantam – 1983

K., Mitchell – The Big Book Goes To Press – The Silkworth Mitchell K. Library – Date Unknown

Kuhar, Michael, Ph.D. – The Addicted Brain – FT Press – 2015

Kurtz, Ernest – Not God – Hazelden – 1991

Mitchel, Dale – Silkworth: The Little Doctor Who Loved Drunks – Hazelden – 2002

Nakken, Craig – The Addictive Personality – Hazelden Publishing – 1996

National Institute on Alcohol Abuse and Alcoholism – Alcohol's Effects on the Body – 2020

Bibliography
(Continued)

Newman, Cory, Ph.D. – Reconciling 12-Step Tenets with Principles of CBT for Substance Abuse Disorder – Beck Institute – 2018

Nowinski, Joseph, Ph.D. – If you work it, It Works – Hazelden Publishing – 2015

Paloutziam, Raymond F. Ph.D. and Park, Crystal L., Ph.D. – Handbook of the Psychology of Religion and Spirituality – The Guilford Press – 2005

Rader, Glenn – STOP – Things You Must Know Before Trying to Help Someone with Addiction – Maze Publishing – 2018

Roth, Fr. Robert J. – William James and Alcoholics Anonymous – America – 1965

SAMSHA – Working Definition of Recovery – A SAMHSA Publication – 2014

Schaeffer, Dick – Choices & Consequences – Hazelden Publishing – 1998

Silkworth, William D., M.D. – Alcoholism as a Manifestation of Allergy – Central Park West Medical Record – 1937

Steigerwald, Fran, M.Ed., and Stone, David, Ph.D. – Cognitive Restructuring and the 12-Step Program of Alcoholics Anonymous – Journal of Substance Abuse Treatment – 1999

Bibliography

(Continued)

The Cabin Group – Understanding and Working AA's 12 Steps using CBT – 2016

Twerski, Abraham J., M.D. – Addictive Thinking – Hazelden Publishing – 1997

Various – Alcoholics Anonymous – AA World Services – 2008

Various – Alcoholics Anonymous Comes of Age – AA World Services – 1957

Various – Pass It On: The Story of Bill Wilson and How the AA Message Reached the World – AA World Services – 1984

Various – The Book That Started It All – Hazelden – 2010

Various – Twelve Steps and Twelve Traditions – AA World Services – 1952

Voxx, Archer – The Five Keys – 12 Step Recovery Without A God – Maze Publishing – 2013

Washton, Arnold M. – Willpower's Not Enough – William Morrow Paperbacks – 1990

White, William L. – Slaying the Dragon – Chestnut Health Systems – 1998

Wilson, Bill – Where Did the 12 Steps Come From? – AA Grapevine – 1953

About the Author

Glenn Rader is an accomplished business professional with a background in organization development and an MBA from the University of Michigan. Mr. Rader is in successful recovery from alcohol and drug addiction and is a public speaker, author, and resource in the addiction recovery community.

Modern 12 Step Recovery is based on the author's participation in Alcoholics Anonymous (AA) and research on the subject. This book was written with the specific goal of making the AA program more accessible to the modern audience seeking recovery from addiction.

Mr. Rader is also the author of the book *STOP – Things You Must Know Before Trying to Help Someone with Addiction*. *STOP* is the product of his work with families and friends of addicts at a major addiction treatment center.

Maze Publishing

Personal Notes

Made in the USA
Monee, IL
26 February 2021